THE THEATRETRAIN WAY

A HANDBOOK FOR DRAMA TEACHERS

By Kevin Dowsett

Layout and design by Demiurge Design
Illustrated by Emma Leahy
Printed by Regal Litho

Photography Credits
David Carver: front cover, 4, 36, rear cover
Richard Washbrooke: 3, 11, 21, 45, 63, 94, 98, 115, rear cover
Chris Christodoulou: 16, 68, 73, 82, 86, 121, rear cover
Phil Pharoah: 18, rear cover.
Emily Withey: 77
Steve Davies: 106
Tony Hart: 112

First published in the UK in 2012 by Theatretrain Ltd.
www.theatretrain.co.uk
British Library Cataloguing in Publication Data:
A catalogue record is available from the British Library
ISBN 978-0-9544289-1-4

Contents

The Theatretrain Way is essentially an interplay between internal thought and outward expression.

INTRODUCTION

The purpose of teaching is to change understanding and see the world in a new way. Good theatre, in whatever form it takes, does this with an audience.

Begin from where you are and what you know. Over a year you discover that this work moves from individual process skills to group production skills. There are different kinds of theatre; individual, small group and local theatre performance to large scale proscenium and arena theatre performance. They all require the same core skills.

As you go along seek these new connections in your work. It is an opportunity to grow as an artist and as a teacher. One of the joys of being a teacher is that you often learn as much as, if not more than, your pupils. Often you learn from your pupils.

If you want to know if you have inspired your pupils then look at them when they leave your class. If they have sparkly eyes and a shiny face the chances are that they have immersed themselves in the work and have been challenged and energised by it. They will take this feeling to their next class; your work feeds the work of others and is cumulative in its effect.

You may not often get thanked as a teacher but you will be rewarded by the changes you see in your pupils as they grow and develop; often wildly beyond what you might have thought possible.

It takes curiosity, time and energy to make work of quality. I hope this guide gives you some creative and inspirational ways to release the imagination of your pupils and helps you to make exciting theatre with them.

Kevin Dowsett
Summer 2012

THE THEATRETRAIN WAY

PROCESS SKILLS

Weekly Class – September to February

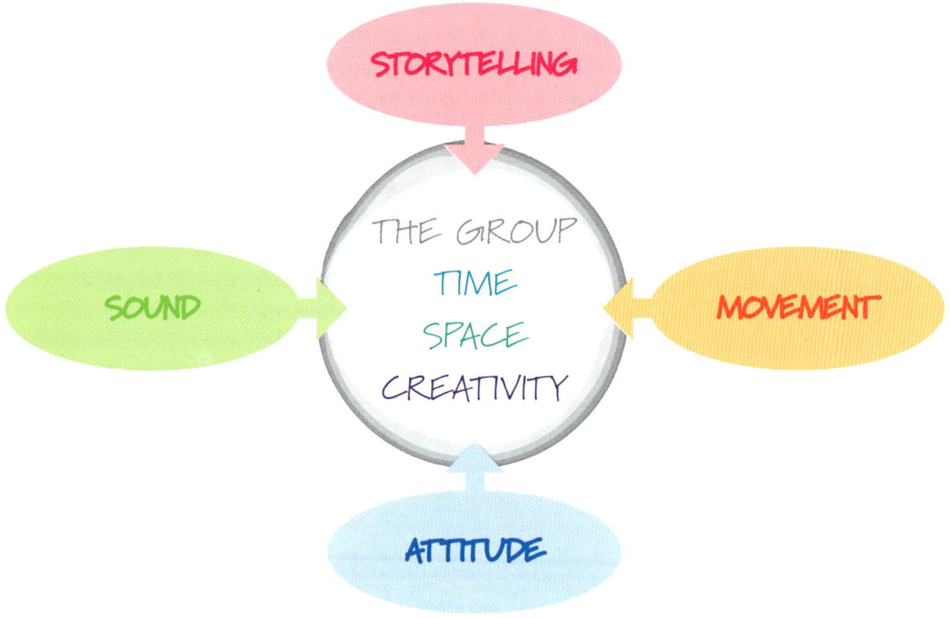

PRODUCTION SKILLS

Weekly Rehearsal – March to July

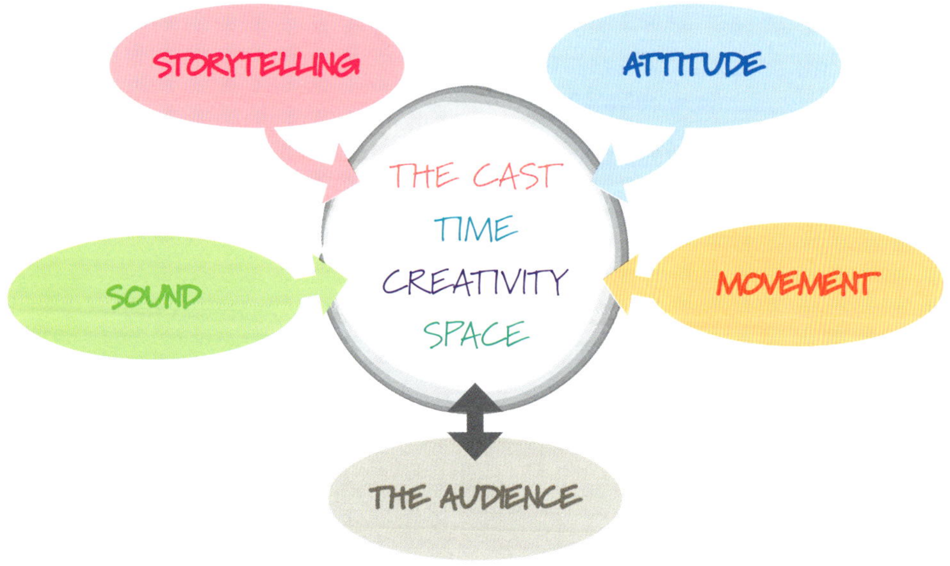

THE THEATRETRAIN WAY

The Theatretrain philosophy has evolved over time and is shown in its simplest form in the above diagram. The skills of drama, dance and singing are interrelated because the primary purpose is to develop an understanding of theatre – i.e. learning the skills of drama, dance and singing and bringing them together for an audience. Each subject has distinct technical skills but in Theatretrain those techniques often cross over in the classroom and in performance. Pupils and teachers are part of a team working towards a common purpose.

There are three essential qualities;

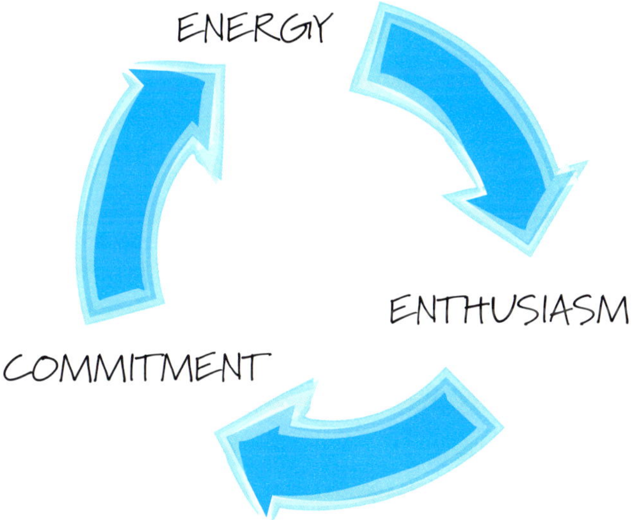

These attributes are necessary to create work of excellence. Without a passion for what you do, your work will not communicate strongly to your pupils, and if you do not project these qualities you run the risk of becoming sloppy, uninspired and cynical.

PROCESS SKILLS

For the first half of each year the work is on process skills in each subject. This is work in groups that focuses on improving the pupils' individual skills in your subject.

THE GROUP The dynamic of the group is vital because it encourages individuals to join their skills to those around them. When you participate in a group you become part of something bigger than yourself. The collective power of dancing, singing or acting reinforces a sense of belonging. Done well, this makes great ensemble theatre and encourages openness in the work. New members grow in confidence because they feel less exposed and quickly join the level of the group. This shared learning is a powerful tool for theatre training and performance.

The work is for children and young people between 6 and 18 years of age divided into 3 age groups.

Although there are three age groups, there are also times when a whole centre works together as one group. A teacher can therefore work with 4 different kinds of groups.

The youngest pupils are between 6 and 9 years of age. Children under the age of 6 are not ready for three hours of classes and they do not usually have the necessary social skills to operate in a group. Aged 6, after a year of school, they are ready to engage with others and focus on the work.

The second group is for those children aged between 9 and 12 years. These are the years of upper primary and lower secondary education. Nine-year-olds can be with the younger or older age group. Some nine-year-olds are happy to be the oldest in the younger group, setting an example and leading the way. Other nine-year-olds prefer the challenge of working with an older age group and following other pupils.

> **TIP**
> Different age groups will bring varying challenges. Be aware of what can be expected within the age groups.

The oldest group is for 13- to 18-year-olds. This age group works against a backdrop of public examinations, relationships, emerging adolescence and the beginning of work in the outside world. They handle more complex techniques and focus on issues more relevant to teenagers.

TIME Each centre operates for three hours, once a week in term time. Each of the three terms runs for about 14 weeks without a break. The 3 age groups have an hour of each subject per week.

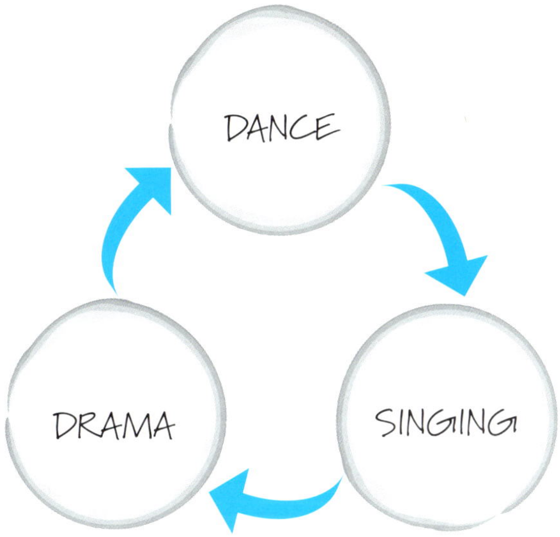

How that time is used is important in the work. The tempo of a class, the timing of a musical number, the pace of a performance are all related to management of time.

SPACE Most centres operate in schools on Saturdays. Dance classes usually operate in the largest space, often with a sprung floor. Drama and singing classes usually use a drama studio or classroom. It is important that there is enough space for the class to move easily and express itself in all subjects. The effective use of space plays an important part in teaching and performing.

CREATIVITY Much of education is given over to instruction. In many dance, drama and music examinations there is a concentration on learning what is necessary to pass. A problem with these examinations is that they tend to examine the examinable and compartmentalise knowledge. They take little account of the imagination and creativity of the individual.

A pupil's energy is connected with their feelings and their understanding of the world. A training achieved by copying a teacher does not give enough space to the imagination of the artist.

The core skills of the Theatretrain Way are...

TIP
These core skills apply to all three subjects

STORYTELLING The central feature of theatre is the story in its many forms. The function of storytelling is to illuminate the world we live in. Done well, it reminds us that life is a universal experience. It explores our hopes, dreams and fears.

SOUND We communicate verbally in speech and in song. There are also other ways of making sound with the body and with objects. Recorded music communicates through rhythm, melody and words.

MOVEMENT Non-verbal communication is expressed by moving the body through time, weight and space. It is an important aspect of drama, dance and singing. The action of singing is a movement and involves expression with the whole body. Dance encompasses a wide range of movement styles and techniques.

ATTITUDE The intensity of emotional feeling that is brought to the work is called attitude. When this is engaged strongly by a group or an individual it creates mood or atmosphere between the participants. If a street dance needs an urban feel then the dancers may need to find an edginess and aggression to their moves. If a singing class is working on "At the End of the Day" from *Les Miserables* they may need to locate a feeling of hunger and anger before they sing.

THE CAST
TIME
CREATIVITY
SPACE

PRODUCTION SKILLS

For the second half of each year each subject works on production skills. Classes become rehearsals and, together with the other teachers, the individual and group skills of the pupils are turned into a performance of high quality.

THE CAST The pupils become a team. They learn their material, commit to what they are doing and give space to others. They take responsibility for what they do individually and as a team and aim to work to the highest possible level.

TIME Rehearsals replace classes and a rehearsal schedule ensures that the work is ready on time. In performance the timing and pace of the material is an important aspect of its success.

CREATIVITY As part of the preparation pupils are taught to “own” the material by understanding the background, context and theme of the story they are preparing. Wherever possible they are encouraged to contribute ideas to the devising of the performance.

SPACE During rehearsals the performance space is marked out and the director/choreographer makes sure that its dimensions are used effectively. The cast are taught to stand by, enter and exit from the performance space. Colour, setting, costume and props play a part in the performance.

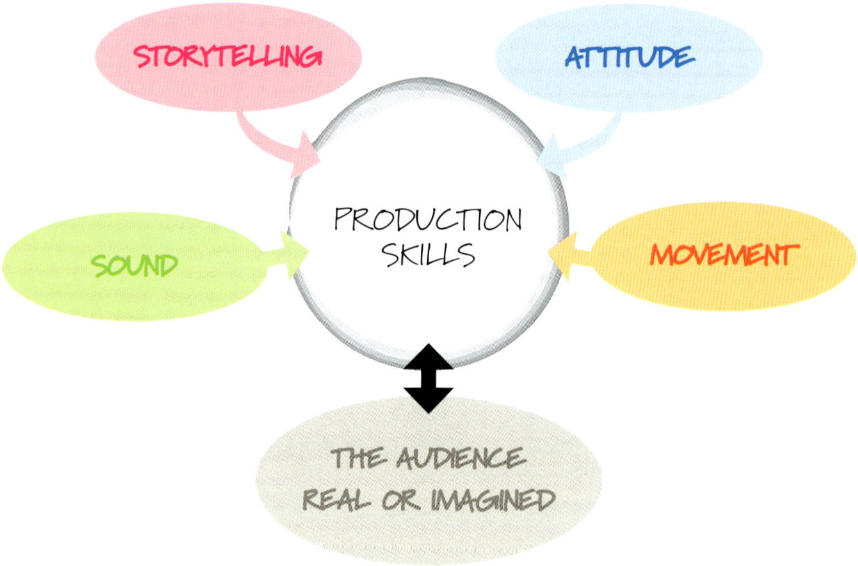

STORYTELLING The whole group is involved in the storytelling. The story must be clear, seen and heard. Conflicts, characterisations or moments of change are emphasised. The work is created in outline and then in detail until it is polished to performance level with all the elements brought together.

SOUND Singing or speaking is audible and shaped to suit the performance. Solos are incorporated into the material and the performers are alive to the moment.

MOVEMENT Movement is sharp and clear with effective use of the body in all its dimensions. The stage picture is dramatic; sometimes with unexpected shapes and structures of group movement.

ATTITUDE Every part of a performance is connected to the world of feelings and emotions. Mood and atmosphere bring a variety of conflicting states including contrast, juxtaposition, chaos and harmony.

THE AUDIENCE During the rehearsals the audience is not present but imagining them and taking account of them is an important part of rehearsal. In later rehearsals the director/choreographer acts as a surrogate audience. In performance a strong connection with the audience is sought.

BEING A TEACHER

Performing arts training adds greatly to young people's lives.

- It allows them to release emotions and feelings.
- The work is immediate and active rather than passive.
- It is shared in a supportive group context.
- Acting out and becoming people in other situations and moods is a good way to understand the world.
- Performing is energising and invigorating and gives a sense of confidence, self-esteem and completion.
- Encouraging creativity releases the imagination and frees the mind.

Introducing the performing arts to young people is a privilege and a responsibility. Done well, it makes a genuine difference to a young person's life; done badly, it can turn a young person off your subject and take away their self-esteem.

Be confident and assertive but also kind and generous. Expect respect from your pupils but in turn respect them and be interested in their progress.

Respond differently to each class in the way that a performer responds to a new audience. Carry the thought that someone in the class may, in time, be better at this than you. Such generosity is life affirming. Your pupils will want to please you if you awaken their curiosity for the work. We all went to school and carry memories of our good and bad teachers. It is a fair bet that your favourite subject was taught by your favourite teacher. It is also likely that you admired that teacher for their energy and enthusiasm and for the atmosphere in their classroom; the way they went about their work.

Inspire creativity by example. Embrace their ideas by adjusting your plans as you go along. You are the catalyst of change for your class; without your intervention, your knowledge and your inspiration the group would not move forward. Be the person who gives them the tools to take their energy, enthusiasm and commitment somewhere worthy of the effort.

TIP

Remember what it was about your favourite teacher that inspired you and gave you enthusiasm for your subject.

This diagram represents the three elements in your classroom/studio. The work exists between you and your class.

Teach the skills of your subject but look for something spontaneous from the individuals before you – something unique to them. Allow your pupils to make some of the decisions in the work. Exploit the creative dynamic between you and the class.

Your life, your knowledge of your subject, your artistic and open-minded nature have given you a point of view which is shaped by your experiences. You decide when to intervene, to challenge, provoke or inspire; you decide when to take a half-formed idea and realise it in a more exciting and complete way. You are the one to step back and see the bigger picture to the work and see it in the context of a term or a year. The more your pupils have ownership of the ideas in the work, the more they will be engaged by it. It will be yours – that is, belonging to all of you. But you are the one to establish the work ethic and the buzz and to lead the way.

NINE ATTRIBUTES OF A GOOD TEACHER

1. Be Organised

Have an aim for every class and a plan for the term.
Teach something new every time.
Manage your time and maximise what can be achieved in an hour.
Vary the work.
Be flexible and open to change.
Use the annual curriculum as a stimulus.

2. Be a Role Model

Be enthusiastic, committed and energetic.
Be kind, generous, fair-minded and receptive to ideas.
Be genuinely interested in the progress of your pupils.

Have a sense of humour.
Be a little apart from your pupils – be the teacher.

3. Be Professional
Be in the room ready to receive your pupils.
Learn their names and use them every week.
Know the health and safety procedures.
Never be alone with a pupil.
Be aware of those who may need special consideration; new pupils, those with illness or family problems.
Be part of the staff team.

4. Have Expectations
Make the work challenging.
Introduce ideas and concepts that deepen the experience.
Pitch the work at an appropriate level for the group.
See their work as part of a journey.

5. Know How to Handle your Groups
Create a supportive, positive atmosphere.
Manage your pupils as individuals but see the work as collective.
Set clear behavioural boundaries and be consistent.
Have a signal for silence; perhaps a clapping rhythm.
Expect them to leave any disagreements at the door.
Have sanctions ready for those whose behaviour is against the ethos of the group.

6. Develop Confidence
Sincerely praise pupils who make progress.
Avoid sarcasm and negativity in your interaction with pupils – it's about them not you.
Welcome mistakes as part of the learning process.
Do not allow pupils to pass judgement on other's pupils' work.
Encourage positive evaluation such as, "Who did good work today?"
Encourage pupils to become leaders and a role model to others.

7. Make the Work Theatrical
Put your work in a theatrical context. Make it different to school.
Mark out a space for each session as a constant in the work.
Use attitude (mood, atmosphere and emotion) to heighten their engagement.

8. Encourage Creativity
Enhance their ideas with your own on-the-spot creativity.
Release spontaneity in them whenever possible.

Dare them to be different as an individual.
Remember material is owned jointly.

9. Evaluate your Work

Evaluate your teaching and their response from week to week.
Take an interest in your own professional and educational development.
Seek out new stimuli to your work – art, poetry, music, films, books, etc.
Attend the annual teacher training sessions.

SOME EXPECTATIONS

Each year the group changes as new people alter its identity. Exploit the changes in the group to bring in new challenges and increase their group sensitivity.

Give the work an emotional content. Expect enthusiasm, commitment and energy in every class. Wake up your pupils to the world and give them work that demands action. Do not be relaxed and laid back. The work is about doing rather than talking about doing. They should be constantly participating in different ways.

There will be times of free uninhibited energy and other times when they are quiet and expected to sense an atmosphere. Use an energetic teaching style. This is not necessarily a physical energy; it can be a mental alertness and concentration. Theatre work requires a sharpness of observation and transformation. Listening and watching skills are part of this process.

Bring intensity to your work; an intensity greater than in normal life. The best theatre is a model of the world; a feeling that it speaks to you and you recognise the truth of it or not. It has a "now" about it – a feeling that it is created before your eyes.

When your class is over your pupils go back to their real world. A week later they come back to the same imaginary place that you create together. It can be comforting to return to a fixed point once a week. For some children it can be an oasis. Make your class different from the everyday experience of learning at school. Be unpredictable, inspiring and fun. Give them something to aspire to. Help them to be brave and overcome obstacles. Encourage them to be generous and thoughtful about others. Teach them to see that we are all on a similar journey and other people are necessary to us. Use spontaneity to keep them on their toes so that their imagination is uninhibited. Expect them to work hard to keep up with the pace of your work.

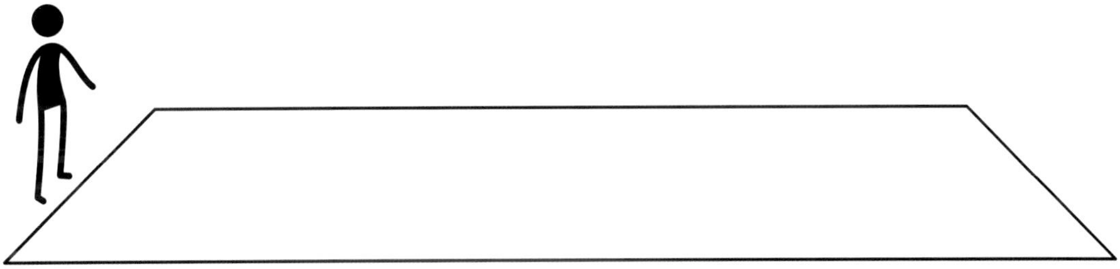

Stepping in and out of the theatre space requires a switch in thinking. They have to attend with concentration and preparation. Put the focus on the work. This is why space plays a key role in establishing a way of working. If you use a marked out theatre space you will define a boundary. It reinforces the sense that it is a special place. If you establish on-stage and off they will discover focus and group alertness - a readiness to perform.

BE READY FOR YOUR CLASS

Do

- Prepare exciting material.
- Plan your work thinking of the response of the least interested person.
- Lay out the room to your agenda.
- Start on time – even if only one has arrived. Latecomers learn to be on time.
- State the aim of the class and make it easy to understand.
- Use supporting material – music, pictures, photographs, diagrams, paper, and pens.
- Move them on with a sense of urgency.
- Draw conclusions from the work.
- Finish on time.

Don't

- Talk too much.
- Allow too much time for discussion.
- Let the pace become too relaxed.
- Use too many games. Once a new skill is mastered, move on.
- Patronise or over-intellectualise.
- Overuse techniques familiar in school drama – hot-seating, thought tracking, etc.

Look for a strong dynamic between the characters

TIME YOUR CLASS

Break your hour-long class into different sections. Keep an eye on the clock.
If necessary use a kitchen timer.

5 MINUTES
Warm up
energy,
engagement

10 MINUTES
Focus and
concentration

15 MINUTES
Introduce the
week's theme

25 MINUTES
Work in different ways:-
As individuals at the same time
As an individual watched by a group
With a partner (twos)
With teacher in role
In small groups – threes or fours
Half the group (other half watching)
The whole group together

5 MINUTES
Brief evaluation
Applause

Allow time and space for pupils to connect to their own thoughts, memories, dreams and imaginations. This might mean that you ask them to sit alone and recall an important event in their life or an imagined place. These simple exercises allow them to realise that acting comes from their head - memories, senses, thoughts or imaginings. They should learn that they are not alone in thinking in this way – that we all share our experience of the world and the theatre is a place where you can bring it to life.

If you work with groups of 3 or 4, talking and listening is necessary as everyone cannot talk at once. Working with a group involves allowing time and space for others, offering up ideas and negotiating and adjusting ideas. You learn that you can't control everything and sometimes you have to follow an idea which you didn't choose or particularly like.

Make learning happen in different ways, mixing the groups and not always allowing friends to work together. Build group spirit by being unpredictable and imaginative with the material, intervening in role or through others to stop work becoming easy or complacent. Think on your feet and incorporate unexpected ideas into the work of the class. Make time for the whole group to be in role together.

Cram a lot of material into a class and prepare more material than you need. If you work at pace and expect the class to keep up with you then you will cover more ground. This need to move on gives the class an edge and a stronger sense of purpose.

At the end of the class an important question to ask is, "Who did good work today?" You can do this by sitting the class in a circle and asking them to point to one person who they thought did well. This immediate selection forces them to think about what has happened. Children and young people are usually fair to each other and usually acknowledge when someone has done well. It reinforces the learning points and adds self-esteem. It also encourages them to be more thoughtful about what they have been doing, to put it in context. Ask individuals why they chose the person they pointed to.

After the class, think about what was achieved in the time and where it should go next.

Ask yourself in all classes

» Can they see your energy, enthusiasm and commitment?
» Are they interested?
» Are you interested in them?
» Is everyone engaged?
» Are you using time efficiently?
» Are you using the space effectively?
» Could the work be more theatrical and exciting?
» Could you stretch them more?
» Are you being spontaneous?

6-9 YEAR OLDS

Do

- Lower yourself to their height.
- Vary your vocal delivery.
- Be ready to join them in role.
- Vary activities to keep their attention.
- Treat them as small adults and they will behave accordingly.
- Encourage them by using stickers and charts sparingly.
- Have expectations – they can achieve more than some people think.
- Take turns and make watching others part of the work.
- Challenge their ideas by intervening in role.
- Make your room a place where they wear some else's shoes.

Don't

- Talk too much about their week.
- Allow a continual procession to the toilet – it means they are bored.
- Talk down to them. They will learn respectfulness from you.
- Allow one or two people to dominate.
- Let the class just play. Give them a purpose and a problem to solve.
- Let cliques develop, vary the working groups.

LEADERS

Among each class will be those who are natural leaders and those who can learn to be leaders. A group benefits from strong characters that are focused and take bold decisions in their work. Encourage confident pupils to lead by example. Good leaders encourage bravery but they do not try to stand out, they blend into the rest of the group and are modest about what they do.

GENEROSITY

There are those who are mean of mind and those who are generous of spirit; givers and takers. Create a harmonious atmosphere in which learning is fun for everyone. The shy feel safe, the exuberant are given space but learn to give others space as well. Demand sensitivity between your performers. By gently valuing openness, friendliness, compassion and sensitivity you will cultivate more creative work and more accepting and interesting pupils.

ENDING A CLASS

- Remind the class of the aim of the lesson.
- Ask what they learnt that was new.
- Sit in a circle and count to three. On three they must point to someone who did good work. Ask one or two people to explain why they chose that person.
- Give your thoughts on what was achieved.
- Applaud the class for their hard work and cooperation.
- Allow them to applaud you for your preparation and skill. Work hard for their applause.

PROCESS SKILLS

Each subject has 5 primary elements:
Time, space, creativity, attitude and storytelling.

Drama has storytelling as a core primary; sound and movement are secondary elements.

Dance has movement as a core primary; storytelling and sound are secondary elements.

Singing has sound as a core element; storytelling and movement are secondary elements.

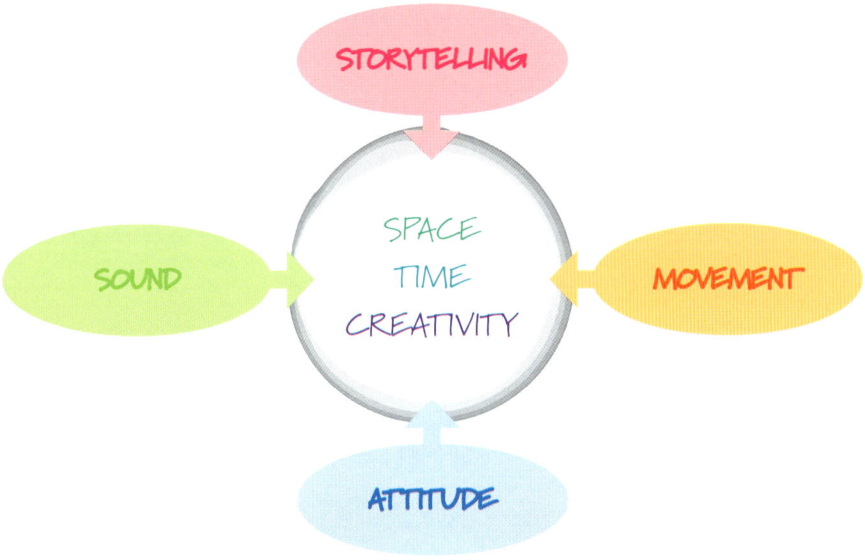

THE ANNUAL THEME

Each year a theme is chosen to bind the work of the three subjects together. Use this theme to unify the storytelling aspect of your work.

Previous themes have included...

- Overcoming the Monster
- Rags to Riches
- The Quest
- Comedy and Tragedy
- Voyage and Return
- Rebirth
- The Dark Figures
- The Light Figures

Storytelling is a teaching area for all three subjects. How you connect to the theme is for you to decide as an individual and as part of a team at your centre. Brief annual notes explain how the theme relates to particular stories. It encourages a new direction for process skills and performance work. Centres often use the year's theme as the theme for their local show.

THE 5 CORE ELEMENTS

1. SPACE Mark out the space so that it is clear what is performing space and what is not. The performers will then be physically connected in the space. Defining the space also makes a separation between the performers and the audience.

Each of us has personal space that surrounds us. This space extends beyond our physical space and is the extent of our reach with all parts of our body at all levels – high, low and medium. To connect our own space with the larger performance space takes time to understand. Pupils need to learn the rules for using stage space effectively.

A singing class is not only about creating a sound. It is creating a shared feeling of a group in the space. How people occupy that space will emphasise the theatricality of what they do.

In dance the placement of the group in the space is often a first decision when creating a performance. We draw conclusions about what we see partly a result of the use of space between and around the dancers.

In acting the differences between characters can be seen from the choices made in positioning as well as how they move.

If space plays an important part in your process work it will make later production work easier. It could be circular

Or rectangular

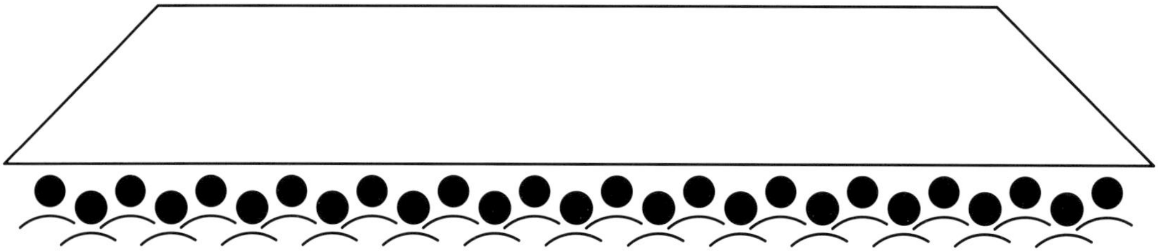

Divide the space in two

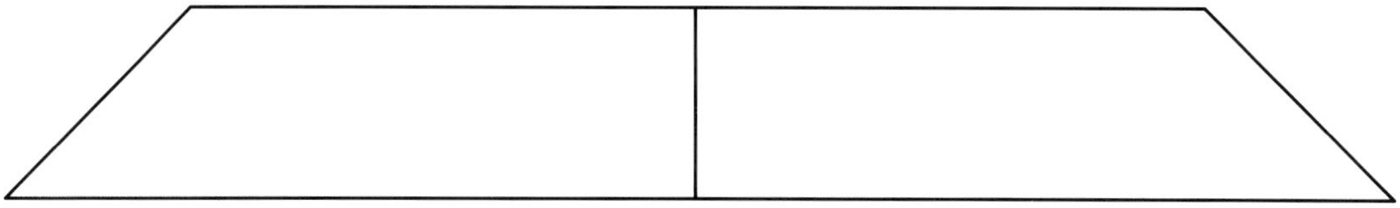

This creates a left and a right.

Divide the depth in two

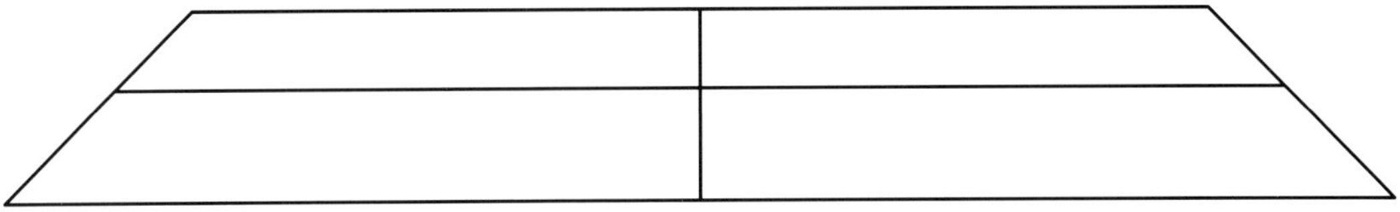

This creates a back and a front (or an upstage and downstage)

Make it three dimensional by using
height and depth.

The centre can dominate the entire space

The edge of the stage may have less power.

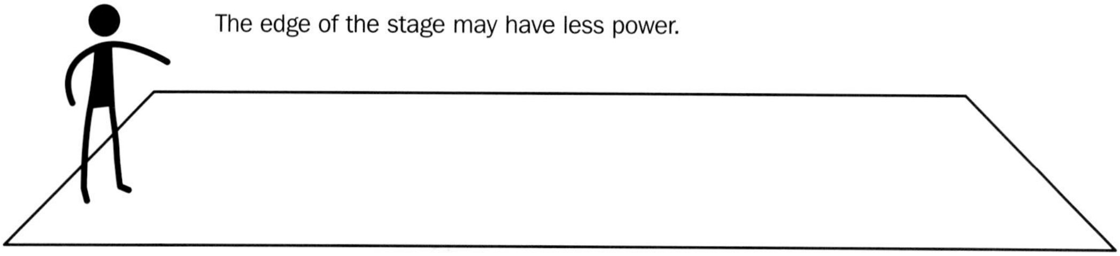

It can be used symmetrically

Or it can be broken up into a less formal structure

There is also the question of how to enter or leave the space.

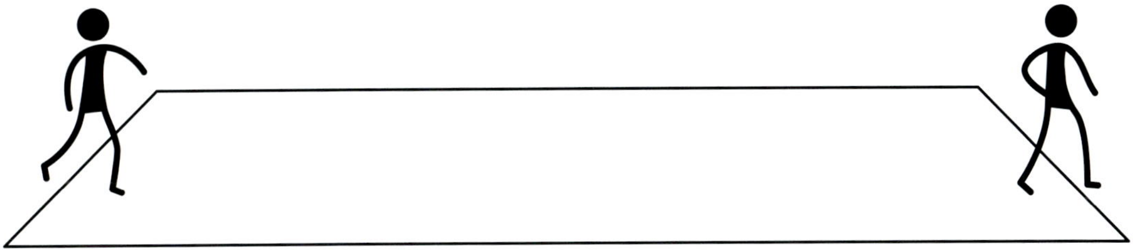

2 TIME Your class is time limited and so is the work that you create. Incorporate a range of tempos and actions. Avoid the tendency for everyone to move at the same speed.

Speeding up
Run, accelerate, canter, gallop, sprint, scamper, hurry, press on, scuttle, scurry, dash, flounce, whisk, rush, bound, bolt, spring, dart, catch up, overtake, leave behind.

Slowing down
Deceleration, creep, crawl, dawdle, linger, loiter, plod, trudge, saunter, lumber, drag, toddle, waddle, shuffle, hobble, limp, totter, falter, stagger, fall behind.

Stopping
Remain, stand, stop dead, freeze, rest, pause, take breath, stagnate, stay, settle, stand still.

Suddenly moving
Impulsive, hurtle, thrust, elbow, charge, tackle, jostle, hustle, shove, collide, clash, strike, knock, whack, pelt, jab, punch, kick, lunge, slog, clout.

Suddenly recoiling
React, spring back, rebound, reverberate, repercussion, rebound, revulsion, ricochet, reflex.

3 CREATIVITY The best way to access your pupils' ideas is to get them to be in role in improvisation. Drama in schools is often a tool used to encourage empathy and to examine social situations for later discussion and reflection. Your work should place the emphasis on human situations and characters through a plot or story; and make the work theatrical. This can take the form of games or exercises but also plays involving the class working with different sized groups or as a whole group working together. Be ready to improvise with your class.

4 ATTITUDE Attitude is the engagement of emotions and feelings in the work. Without this connection the work could be superficial and shallow. Create a palette to draw upon by using different emotions and feelings in the work. Begin with the basic emotions of

Taken from Robert Plutchik's 'Wheel of Emotions', 1980

When you introduce attitude in the work you give it immediacy. It is exhilarating to perform with the power of an emotion. It makes the work sharper and more energised. Build stronger attitude between the performers by emphasising the conflicts between the forces represented on stage. The world is in a constant struggle between conflicting states. In the physical world there is light and shade, hot and cold, liquid and solid. The human world has male and female, love and indifference, strength and weakness. (Appendix B lists many more of these opposite qualities). Seek out these contrasts in the work.

Performers should be alive when they perform; their work should live powerfully in the space. If a performer does not know who they are and what they are doing then they will not be connected to what is going on around them.

Finding the conflict in a piece of drama touches rawer emotions. The struggle can be between two people or opposing thoughts, or tribes or between the performers and the audience. All stories have a struggle – often between characters that are simply good or bad. If the conflict lacks bite it can be made more apparent through attitude.

5 STORYTELLING This area of your work is concerned with learning the skills of improvisation and creating a character. Younger pupils enter a role easily; older pupils are taught skills such as playing objectives, strategies, status, learning about the given circumstances of the situation and the previous history of the character.

Storytelling also involves devising ideas and creating scenes and stories and giving them a shape and structure.

SECONDARY ELEMENTS (IN DRAMA)

SOUND Storytelling often involves speech as part of creating a character. It can be developed and shaped. Warm-ups and exercises should involve speech work and release energy through sound. The group should have opportunities to make sounds together such as chanting or soundscapes.

MOVEMENT The relationships between people on stage are movements in time and space. Rudolph Laban's movement theories (with a combination of time, space, weight and flow) are an easy-to-use movement vocabulary. Physicality is an important part of developing a character. Again, exercises and games play a part in this process.

A Summary

In the first six months of the year you

- Rebuild the group and absorb new pupils.
- Share new skills and techniques.
- Focus on a theme through storytelling.
- Incorporate movement, sound and attitude as a natural and important part of your work.
- Focus on time and space skills as other key elements.
- Use conflict to give the work a dramatic edge and relate this to movement, sound, space and particularly attitude.
- Give your pupils a sense of gradual development of their skills, a confidence in new things and a strong sense of belonging to the group.
- Expect your pupils to be creative with the work, to bring something of them to what they do.

TEACHING PROCESS SKILLS

CORE SKILLS

- **CREATIVITY** being in role and improvising, having ideas.
- **STORYTELLING** becoming a character, exploring the theme.
- **SPACE** using stage space effectively.
- **TIME** varying the tempo of the work.
- **ATTITUDE** finding the conflicting atmospheres and feelings of the characters.

SECONDARY SKILLS

- **SOUND** harnessing voice work and other sources of sound.
- **MOVEMENT** developing a movement vocabulary.

FURTHER SKILLS INCLUDE

Working with scripts

Mini Projects

Stage combat

Masks

CORE SKILLS - CREATIVITY

Learning to be in Role

The youngest age group use role play as part of their lives; it is how they understand the world.

Do

- Join them in role whenever possible.
- Manipulate the plot to exploit the theatrical possibilities of a story.
- Play a secondary character yourself and encourage those who stand back to take a greater part in the story.
- Think on your feet and extend ideas in new directions. If you have a group of boys playing pirates who always want to have a sword fight then deepen their work. Investigate what happens if someone gets wounded or is fatally hurt? Ask some of them to give the bad news to the family. Follow through the consequences of actions but retain what they find fun.
- If necessary come out of role and talk about the situation before continuing.

You may find yourself saying....

"When we start can you believe that I am someone else?"
"And so are you."
"Help the story and allow other people to play their part."
"Sometimes we need to take turns."
"Silence and wondering what to do next may be part of the story."
"All of us are making this story, not just a few."
"You need to be in the same story as everyone else and not go off on your own."

As children grow up their use of improvisation becomes more sophisticated. Older pupils are used to working in groups and discussing things before they start improvising.

Do

- Put a time limit on discussion to encourage spontaneity. Get them used to creating in a short period of preparation. Get them on their feet early.
- Sometimes give them an idea and start without discussion.
- Challenge individually the different personalities in the group.
- Get them to go beyond stereotyping of characters. Help them to find an authentic personal voice in what they do.
- Use music and physicality in the work and develop an ensemble style.

- Work on situations which they are likely to have experience of as well as experiencing life from another person's point of view. What they would do if the events were happening to them?
- Encourage them to leave their comfort zone.
- Aim to build a group with mutual trust and the confidence to deal with themes sensitively.
- Get them to suspend their disbelief and enter into the imaginary pretext of a scene.

Don't

- Let discussions become so protracted that they never begin the scene.
- Allow pupils to trivialise the work or constantly invent characters and situations that make a joke of everything.
- Create work too freely from television. Find more exciting and immediate forms.

THE BASIC SKILLS OF IMPROVISATION

Establish ways of working for your different age groups. They should:-

- Believe in the situation and work positively with those around them.
- Watch other people's work and be a good audience.
- Collectively create atmosphere, a spell which they should not break.
- Understand that the work is not only about them but everyone in the group.

Teach them to be open, creative and spontaneous. One of the best books about improvisation is Keith Johnstone's *Impro*. He explains how improvisation works and how you can develop it in class. At the centre of his work is the concept of making *an offer* when someone begins a scene. He explains that the other actor(s) need to *accept* the offer to build a scene. Some performers *block* the offer or accept the offer in a way that kills the scene. He suggests games and improvised scenes to encourage creative openness, make you aware of blocking and become more generous and positive as a performer. By using Keith Johnstone's theories you can recognise what is happening and lead your pupils to an atmosphere of greater fun, creativity and self belief.

Change the Scene

The group sits in a circle. The first person (A) enters the space and carries out a task (say, painting a fence). The next person (B) enters the space and says something ("Can you tell me where the cinema is?" Would be a dull but acceptable choice). A forgets the fence painting and serves the needs of B by keeping the scene going. "Oh yes, it's the first on the right" would be a dull acceptance of the offer; more exciting would be, "I'll show you. Are you going to see *Dracula*?" This would accept the offer and in turn be making another offer and advancing the scene.

Everyone can have a go and, as no one knows how the next person will change the scene, it is unpredictable. A creative group can delight in making highly unusual offers which are taken up in ever more unusual ways.

You can also develop the game by having the second person come from anywhere in the circle but pick up on an action they can see A making. For instance the painting of the fence could be interrupted by B swishing away flies saying,"They drive you mad don't they? I use spray."

TIP
Some pupils will become spectators if you let them. Encourage everyone to join in

Vary the group size to be less predictable.

Scenes for 2 people

6-9s	An ugly duckling grows into a swan.
9-12s	A teacher keeps a pupil behind to talk to them.
13-18s	"What have you been saying behind my back?"

Scenes for 2 people against 1

6-9s	The nasty step brothers or sisters demand that a younger sibling wait on them. Revenge is sweet!
9-12s	Playing mum off against dad to get what you want.
13-18s	Two people were best friends until a new person came along.

Scenes between 3-4 people

6-9s	The naughty children, the glue and what happened to them.
9-12s	Standing up to a bully.
13-18s	Peer pressure – smoking, drinking or antisocial behaviour.

Scenes for the whole class

6-9s:	Goldilocks is interviewed about what happened to her.
9-12s	What happens when someone runs away from home? Multi viewpoints.
13-18s	"The new motorway means your homes will have to be demolished."

CORE SKILLS - STORYTELLING

This is at the centre of your work and gives it unity and structure.

Creating a Character

A character is an imaginary person who may or may not be like the actor. They are often trapped in a situation which is difficult for them. They have a past which has made them what they are and they are driven to try and get what they want in their life.

Character and plot are integral because the one gives context to the other. It can be set now or in the past, here or in other times and other places – even fairy tales for younger pupils. Expect your pupils to work with specific details and avoid generalising; what Stanislavski would call the *given circumstances*. Carefully set up the who, the where and the when – even in a simple story.

A character behaves the way they do for a reason. Make it clear that this is called an objective. Put simply, it is what the character wants. It is what drives them.

- Robin Hood wants justice for the poor people of Nottingham.
- Cinderella wants to go to the Ball.
- James Bond wants to succeed in his mission.
- Juliet wants her Romeo.

By overcoming obstacles we see their true character emerge.

Work in pairs (A and B)

Tell A and B that they are old friends from school days and are meeting for coffee.

Then give more information secretly to the As then the Bs. This will create a conflict and an unexpected frisson to the scene.

Tell A that they always liked B and have missed them. They are using this get-together as an opportunity to become closer friends again.

Tell B that they have moved on from A. They are happy to meet but they don't want a future friendship.

Without planning anything the whole class should launch into the scene at the same time.

Watch some of the results and talk about the tactics used as each character tries to reach their objective. What strategy does A use to become friendlier? How does B discourage them? People are more interesting when they use unexpected means of getting what they want. Most people want something from someone else. It could be wealth, fame, approval or disapproval. Knowing what your character wants is a key factor in bringing them to life.

As your young actors become more aware of the conflict between the characters you can increase the tension between them. This dynamic can be the most satisfying part of acting because they can use tactics to try and control events – tactics that will vary according to what happens as they go along.

Tell A to borrow something (it could be money) from B.

Tell B to be unwilling to lend to A as they have done so before and it took a long time to get it back. What happens next? A might start off by praising B or making them laugh and putting them in a good mood. B might sense what is coming and may feel they are being softened up. They might be polite but non committal. When A asks B for the money B might be offhand and vague about it.

The scene is a tug of war between two people who are both trying to get what they want from each other. A may have created an atmosphere in which it is difficult for B to deny them. On the other hand B may be so unfriendly and distant and develop an atmosphere that is unwelcoming and brittle. A might try to manipulate B to make them feel guilty. "You are the only person I can ask. You know I've had a difficult time. I wouldn't ask you if you weren't my best friend." Or even, "Go on then. Forget it. I shouldn't have asked you. It's fine. Just leave me, I'll be alright." (said while wiping away a tear).

This jockeying for position between the protagonists is fun to do and to watch, each trying to outdo the other. When your actors can play such scenes they learn to listen and respond to each other.

More conflict scenarios to be resolved...

- A teenager persuading their strict mother to let them go to a sleepover.
- A motorist trying to talk a traffic warden out of giving them a ticket.
- A pupil trying to get a teacher to let them off a detention.
- A trainee fairy persuading their sorcery teacher to teach them magic spells.
- A son or daughter trying to persuade a parent to let them have a dog.
- A child attempting to get their parent to raise their pocket money.

You can create scenes by having A and B interact as brothers and sisters or as flatmates. Ask them to begin the scene to establish their relationship. Interrupt and call out two random attributes from the human qualities list in APPENDIX B. The list is not a list of emotions but of adjectives – the actor brings in the new mood or atmosphere that you have asked for. You can choose words at random. Each character has to try and keep their mood strong enough to influence the other.

When they get good at playing this exercise expect them to find a reason to change the emotion you have given them. A may be dreamily and romantically gazing at B while B is bored, yawning and flicking through magazines. When new titles are announced of "crying" and "laughing", A may begin to cry because the love they feel for B is not returned – or better still because they love them so intensely. On the other hand, B may begin to laugh at what they see as ridiculous attention-seeking behaviour. By moving from one mood to another they justify their change in the other person's behaviour. Audiences love the switchback and erratic behaviour of such "flatmates", and when watched it often seems surprising truthful.

Interject solo work into a class. Teach them that acting is partly about understanding the self in relation to the world around us. We all have to balance the inner private self with the outer public self. It can be effective to have them use a sense memory of a particular time and place to deepen their individual response in the work.

Working on Objectives

This is a class for older pupils investigating the connection between thinking and acting.

1) Ask for everyone to work in groups of 3. Each person in the group labels themselves A, B or C.

Ask them to listen only to what they are required to do.

A loves (likes) B

B loves (likes) C

C loves (likes) A

But also ...

A hates C

B hates A

C hates B

This introduces objectives or intentions. We are all driven by what we want from a situation. Watching a character trying to achieve their objective makes them interesting to us. Even if they do not succeed, their action of trying engages us. You may need to stop the action and suggest some tactics.

2) The next exercise takes this ABC of storytelling and playing objectives to a different level. Choose three people; if possible two girls and a boy. Explain that A and B are a couple and have been seeing each other for about 6 months. C is a stranger to the couple who has never seen them before. The scene takes place at a house where a party is being held – specifically the bedroom where the coats are stored. A final piece of information is that when the couple entered the house C looked at the boy and he looked at her and they liked what they saw!

Those are the given circumstances. Ask them to leave the room and come back in, one at a time, to receive further secret information. In life you don't always have the full information about someone and this new layer of information will complicate the situation.

One by one they return and the rest of the class hears the extra information given to each character.

A is the girlfriend. Recently she has been bored by their relationship and considered ending it. However the other night she had a dream where the boyfriend had a central and romantic role. She woke up realising that she loved him and is now fearful of losing him. She is using this party as an opportunity to get closer and to let him know how much he means to her. However, when she walked in she couldn't help noticing that C made eye contact with him across the

room. Begin the scene in the room by talking to him and telling him how happy he makes her.
Objective: to keep this relationship alive.

B is the boyfriend. Recently his relationship has been going nowhere and he has decided to end it. However, A has been making such a big deal about this party that he didn't want to let her down tonight. He is a nice guy and doesn't like causing a scene. However, when he walked into the party he saw a stranger (C), and as soon as their eyes met he was interested. B doesn't know if C is interested in him. If there was any way that B could find out C's phone number he might be able to tell her he was interested. But he is careful not to be mean or thoughtless to A.
Objective: to be polite but if possible find out if C is interested in you.

C is the other girl. She does not know anyone at this party and is bored. She saw the couple come in and was instantly interested in B. She is also sure that he is interested in her even though he is with A. She wants to find out more. She sees them go into the room with the coats but they don't come out. She decides to wait a while to let them chat and then go in to see what is happening and listen to what they are saying. She invents a pretext to go in.
Objective: to see if the boy is interested in you.

As each character is given their extra information they are asked to go back outside and keep these details to themselves

They begin the scene with the couple entering the room.

3) Ask A, B and C to sit next to each other and explain that you are going to run the scene again; but with a difference. Ask for three volunteers and each volunteer stands behind one of the characters. They are going to voice the character's thoughts. Explain that each voice has two points of view which they can voice as many times as they like. Thoughts cannot hear each other and they hang in the air unheard by anyone.

A's voice. Remind them that they love B and give full voice to how wonderful it is to be with them with all the depth of feelings for them. (You need a brave pupil for this role.) The other side of their character is a hatred directed towards C who they instantly spot as a threat. They can be as hate-filled as they like towards them; they can't hear them.

B's voice. Remind them that they are disinterested in this relationship and looking for a way out. On the other hand when the stranger enters it might be,

"Well hello, I like the look of you!"

C's voice. One side is very interested in the boy and the other is a hate-filled rant directed at the girl.

Ask each character to work as a partnership between the voice and the body. The voice can stand anywhere in the room although it is better if they can see their partner's face. If A looks at another character then their "thought" voice could pick up on that and supply a new train of thought. This could be very subtle work. When you begin you may find that either they speak all at once and nothing gets heard or they have nothing to say. The "moving" actors have little to say and communicate mainly through gesture and body language.

It becomes fascinating to watch as a multi-layered tumble of actions, reactions, thoughts and inner voices from sad and poetic to rude and aggressive. The tension between people behaving politely towards each other and the reality of their feelings can be very dramatic.

4) When this has been completed there is another level of exploration. Keep the same original actors but change the voices. This time the "thoughts" are asked to express their feelings not through words but through actions and you play a dramatic piece of music to set a mood of tension.

A's inner thoughts. Express their love of B with as many actions of love that they can think of; blowing kisses, dancing towards them, directing their hands from their heart, going on one knee and proposing, etc. They can go close to the real character but cannot touch them as they are a thought but not a reality. Their hatred of C can be expressed through any dramatic movement to kill off their rival. They might stab them, blow them up, poison them, shoot them, fire arrows, hang them, fire a huge canon, etc.

B's inner thoughts. Express their need to escape the relationship by looking for but never finding the way out of the room – they are trapped. On the other hand they can express their interest for the stranger in many flirtatious and romantic ways.

C's inner thoughts – varied forms of death and hatred to A and adoration, love and future happiness with B.

Each character is played realistically by the "moving" actors (who this time use no words) and the thoughts who each have a double set of moves and gestures towards their love or hate. Each character is lost in their own world; a world which does not connect with the others. And the thoughts have intentions which are double edged.

5) If there is time you can ask for three more volunteers who have not yet had a turn. Again you play music but this time it can be heroic (or mock heroic) and the characters wear white neutral masks. Their intention is to mock the original story. It should be as exaggerated and ludicrous as possible.

The Given Circumstances

Human beings are contradictory. They don't always reveal what they are thinking. This makes them endlessly fascinating. The dynamics between the characters and how they are affected by events is what keeps us watching.

Ask the following questions of a character...

- Who am I?
- When is this happening?
- Where am I?
- What do I want?
- What am I doing?
- Why?

Pupils have to learn to be specific about what they are doing. If you agree the given circumstances, even in a simple form, it will sharpen their sense of the character.

Create solo work based on the above questions and set it at a park bench. Present some of the solos and ask the group if they think they can tell the who, the why and the what from the behaviour of the character.

Entering and Leaving the Space

They say when we meet someone new we judge them within 10 seconds. It is an instinctive reaction based on appearance and speech. Often people will say later "I knew they were like that – from the first time I saw them." A first entrance is therefore a potent place to encapsulate a character's intention. If you give characters a reason to enter or exit they become more interesting and the actor is less self-conscious. Have your actors be in role before they enter rather than enter and then become. Show the difference to them.

Try some of these entrances:

- A thief slipping into a changing room to steal money.
- A couple returning home to find their house has been burgled.
- A person entering for a job interview but finding no one there.
- Snow White entering and eating the poisoned apple.
- A mother entering the room of a child who has gone away.

And some of these exits:

- A thief slipping away after stealing.
- A teacher leaving the classroom at the end of a day.
- A prisoner leaving their cell on the day of release.
- A worker going home for the last time on the day of retirement.
- A couple leaving their house for the final time.

Sharpen the Work

As a performer you may have had the experience of being in the moment; a heightened sense of being so focused on a situation that everything else recedes and you forget where you are. To encourage this level of consciousness choose material that has high stakes for the characters and a strong sense of conflict between two opposing sides. Once someone responds to the atmosphere in this way it will affect other people and deepen the work.

TIP
Use the door of the room to make a scene more real.

Do

- Cut a scene short if there is no development of character and situation. Some will be indulgent with time if you let them. Get to the point and move on.
- Demand that they use real objects in a scene. If a door is needed use the one in the room.
- Secretly tell someone to enter a scene with new information.
- Enter a scene yourself in character with some news.
- Engineer unexpected developments to keep them on their toes.
- Demand of characters who are flagging, "What do you want?" They should be able to tell you their objective without thinking.
- Play music to heighten the emotion.
- Think about how they could make the conflict and physicality clearer and more deeply felt.

In a scene between two people in deep disagreement, whisper to one of the actors to leave the room. This usually surprises the person who is left. Side coach them by saying, "Well do you want to sort this out or not?" If they still look helpless say, "Well you could go after them." If they chase after the first actor take the rest of the class along to watch. This increases the tension as everyone is intrigued to see how it will play out. Often the intensity between the performers becomes highly charged or intimate as a different space brings a different atmosphere. It seems closer to reality.

Use the advantage of secrecy. By giving information to characters and withholding it from others you encourage unpredictability. Surprise them by changing the order of what you do. If a particular scene intrigues you, allow it to develop and introduce more complications, perhaps involving the whole class in it. Some film directors use this technique, keeping the cameras rolling at the end of a scene to see what will happen. This sense of unknown territory will keep your actors on their toes and stop complacency setting in. Gently guide them to more interesting solutions.

Drama deals with the difficult situations in life. A feeling of well-being and pleasure is not enough; it looks at a man or a woman, a boy or a girl in a mess. This is as true of Little Red Riding Hood as it is of James Bond.

More things you can say to make your studio a more creative place. Say

- "Expect the unexpected."
- "The scene isn't over until I say."
- "Go on" (said when they think they have finished).
- "They meet again six months later having not spoken to each other. Go."
- "If you feel uncomfortable that is probably how the character feels so it's fine."
- "Yes" or "Good" (or make affirmative sounds when you think a good decision has been taken, "Aha" or " Mm.").

When you are watching their work make your focus total and use the audible sounds mentioned above to encourage imaginative spontaneous choices as they go along. This positive instant feedback will encourage them to be more alive. The class will be intrigued by your interplay with the actors. It will stop them breezing through the material it as if everything in life is already set out and easy.

Use Status

Differing status between characters provides another area of conflict. Keith Johnstone describes some excellent examples and games in his books (*Impro: Improvisation and the Theatre* and *Impro for Storytellers: Theatresports and the Art of Making Things Happen*). Use status as a way of differentiating characters and their relationship to each other. Do this in the youngest age group by asking them to make a line with the tallest at one end and the shortest at the other, or the oldest at one end and the youngest at the other. Exaggerate the characters in the youngest age group and let kings, queens or rulers have their own space, speak in a special voice and add to their importance with servants and advisors.

Explain that status works best if the characters acknowledge each other's status. With older pupils gaps in status can be narrower and more subtle. There are many status games that help them to be more alive to each other.

You could act out a true historical event. King Richard II sat on the throne talking to no one but watching everyone. If his eye fell on anyone in particular they had to bend their knee towards the King.

The fun is in behaving towards others as you think the status requires.

Another variation is to ask a group of 5 to decide each person's status. We watch them at a party and try to work out who is high and who is low.

Ask the older group to stand in a circle and in a neutral status position. Straight up with weight equally balanced, chin slightly up, hands hanging loosely by the side, returning eye contact easily. It is a surprisingly difficult thing for some people to do. Varying status from high to low with body language, posture, voice and gesture should be a natural part of your work with them.

TIP
Keeping your chin slightly raised will affect your status

Newspaper and sellotape can make interesting costumes

Building a Character's Past

The purpose of this exercise is to understand how a character feels, to see how an incident in character's past can be explored – in a scene that potentially involves everyone in the class.

- Ask the actor to invent an event that happened to them (the character) that may have an important bearing on their behaviour in the scene and may even explain it. It should be a moment of real significance to them. Use your judgment to decide whether the chosen moment is really going to help them.
- When they have described the event (and it must be one that involves other people) explain that you are going to act out this moment using the whole group in an improvisation. It may involve things that are unexpected for them but they should continue and see what happens. Remember the purpose of this improvisation is to give that actor/character a strong sense of how the character feels at one important moment in their life. That may not be clear until the exercise has finished.
- When the episode is decided upon and described to everyone, send the actor out of the room to wait. Then think quickly. Set up the group to bring the story to life so that when the actor renters the room it is already happening. It is best to involve the whole class in this improvisation but it may be an incident involving only two other people. Try to invent roles for other people. They could be "walls" to the room, members of the community such as neighbours, etc, or even consciences or spirits. You do not have to be too literal but you should give a clear sense of purpose to everyone. You are heightening the event and raising the emotional stakes. If it is a situation where they are 'put down' by someone then choose someone who is good at that. Give some brief background so everyone is agreed on the time and place and an order of events. The group will build the atmosphere. If a fight is in the story think of an imaginative solution, maybe by making it a verbal or slowing down the action and having the group make sounds. You and the group (and key individuals) map out a simple and easy-to-remember storyline. Get one person to start things off and then build a chain of events. Different people can come in at different points – even changing their character.

  If the event is about a girl telling a boy that she wants to finish with him, then begin it happily. Make it a party, play some music and have a good time. Start in one mood and move to another. Exploit a changed mood.

  Tell the group to watch you out of the corner of their eye because you don't want them to just make up a play (some of them get carried away if they are on the edge of the action). Remind the group that the purpose of this improvisation is to benefit one actor.

- Begin. When they re-enter the room they find that the furniture has been moved around and the scene is already happening. They may be thrown because they thought that they would be making all the decisions. This is more like real life, where you must deal with things as you go along

  Control events when the actor re-enters by directing beyond the eye line of the actor. You can stand behind the actor and beckon to the group towards the actor. You could get them to slowly stick their finger out to him or her. You could direct them all away to sit down and suddenly the actor is alone again. If you were discreet the actor would have no idea that you were controlling it.

  Create easy-to-understand signals for; go away, sit down, stand, raise your hands, come closer, surround them, stare at them, faster, slower, be silent, etc. The collective pressure of the group is very powerful in this exercise.

  You could whisper to an actor to bring something new to the story or tell an actor (without being seen) to leave the action. Think on your feet and make the scene focused on what the actor originally said it was about – what actually affected them. Some is decided quickly in advance and some is decided as it unfolds.

  If you have chosen the actors well they will make a strong start and the story will force the character to deal with something difficult. Sometimes the character has to think and not say much in the scene. Other times they are talking about something very emotional. By dramatising their story you fix a stronger sense of it in their mind.

  The possibility of altering things as they go along means you have several opportunities for deepening the idea they first gave you.

- The exercise ends with the actor/character left alone. This is important and easy to set up. You can engineer the other characters to leave a scene and you explain this at the set up. If the whole group surrounds the actor it is easy for you to motion them to sit down. If they are a responsive group, they will follow each other and quietly disappear. When the character is alone introduce music to touch the mood of the scene. Create a contemplative atmosphere for the character/actor to remain in alone. Be prepared to use different kinds of music to draw upon. Select something that seems appropriate for the mood. It is not important that they know or even like the music.

  So everything is directed at the actor to help them realise, often in an unexpected way, the "previous circumstances" of the character. There is no need to discuss it after. It is a personal to them and their character and not for the group. The group's purpose was to help but they usually have great fun as well.

- By the time you start the next one you should find the group itching to go with a new scene and a different atmosphere. Once you have done one or two, you and group will get better at working this way and it won't take as long to set up. They realise that acting is about working together to create something and this exercise is a great way to bond actors and make them care about the characters they are playing. It makes a great company atmosphere.

At the start tell the actor that they are not allowed to leave the room or to end the scene. Some people don't like being on the hook and will give themselves an ending. You want them to be on the hook. Sometimes a character is alone and nothing is being said and they don't know what to do next so they want to end it. But life isn't like that. Like it or not you have to carry on and it's good for them to learn that. Use your discretion to check that it does not become too much for them.

The middle age group should have a very simplified version of the above. Imagined scenes from the past life of the characters would be useful for them to investigate the characters. The 6-9 age group are not ready to work in this way and gain more from understanding the story more fully.

This is a creative way of working with your pupils with the bonus of making you creative as well. It is exciting to be working entirely spontaneously and often happy accidents or unexpected discoveries are made. If you work in this way a lot you will discover that there are a number of incidents that recur in people's previous life experiences. Bullying at school, the end of a relationship with either a parent or a partner, a death, the best day of someone's life, being caught doing something you shouldn't, being accepted as part of a bigger group, being ostracised from a group, causing pain or suffering to others. These themes play on people's minds and set them on a road that can be positive or negative. The skill that you need to develop as a teacher is to quickly sense the crux of the dilemma that is described and then heighten its potential for theatre so they get a strong sense of being in that person's shoes.

Devising

Storytelling also involves creating ideas for characters and situations and making structures to communicate ideas. Devising is a natural part of improvisation.

Do

- Introduce the structure of stories; beginning, middle, end.
- Build the journey section by section.
- Examine stories from a thematic point of view – why this story now?
- Use different events and rhythms to juxtapose and vary the tempo.
- Use tension as a way of tightening or releasing the mood.
- Create a climax to the action.
- Make physicality as important as words.
- Explore ensemble ways of putting the ideas together – song, music, movement, poetry, masks, mass movement, total theatre.
- Find new styles and genres to represent stories.

CORE SKILLS - SPACE

Spatial Awareness

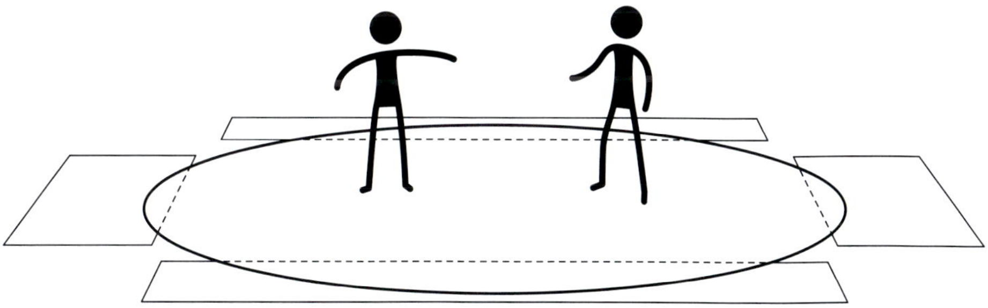

In the round

Proscenium

Thrust

Traverse

Probably the most familiar theatre space is the proscenium stage. In the classroom this is an easy space to recreate. It is rectangular and at its simplest you can represent it by standing a chair in each corner. It is also easy to mark out with tape or string. Defining the space creates an atmosphere for rehearsal and the concentration and focus that are required. It imposes a set of rules.

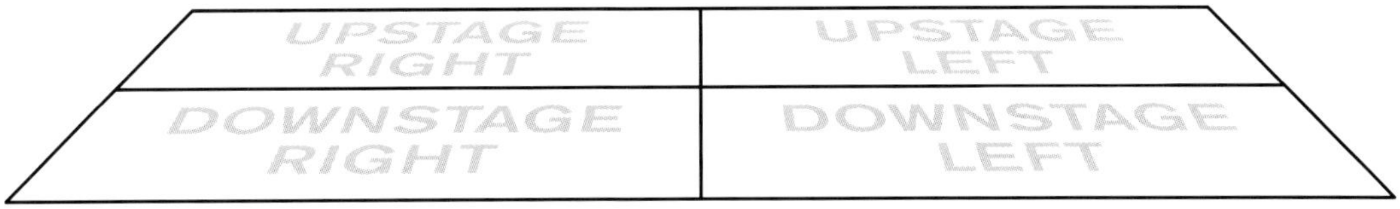

1) Divide the stage space in sections to create an upstage and downstage and stage left and right (the actor's direction when facing the audience). With younger pupils mark out these sections and turn them into rooms or spaces where different emotions live. They can travel from the happy box to visit the sad or angry or scared box. By becoming aware of the space as a set of smaller spaces they can learn how spaces relate to each other. 6-9 year olds take time to operate effectively in space so give them plenty of opportunity to do so.

- Play games related to confined space.
- Exploit the centre of the space which is often the most powerful position.

Explore the concept of symmetry by asking one person to stand anywhere except the centre and have the next person balance the space by standing in the appropriate adjacent place to achieve symmetry. When the person has decided everyone else can give their opinion.

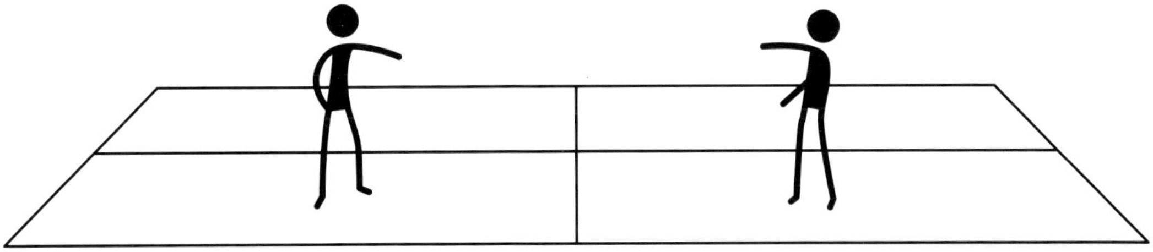

Space is balanced left to right but not front and rear

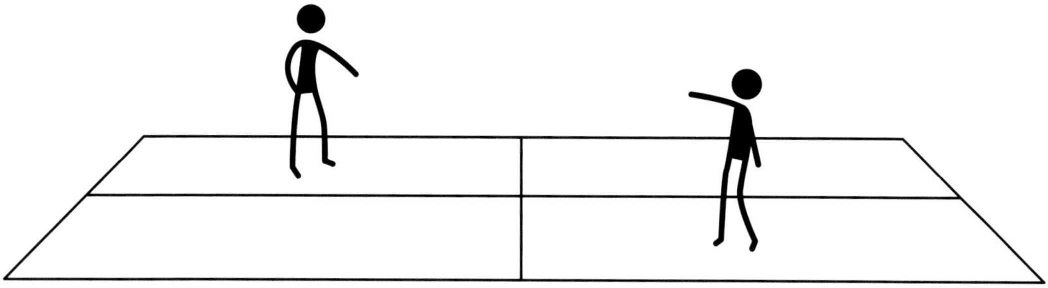

Balanced left and right and front and rear

2) Once this has been mastered, complicate things by asking one person to stand where they like but ask two people standing together to balance the space. How the balance is made is a personal choice. If you regarded the first example above as a seesaw they would topple, so how could they counteract that? Perhaps one higher and one lower would balance. Have the two volunteers speak aloud as they decide what to do and then give everyone else a chance to express their point of view.

3) With older pupils have the first person express an emotion with their pose. The second person looks at the shape and balances the emotion in the space. Would their choice be a complementary feeling or one of opposition?

By adding more people to the picture you can balance one person with, say, a group of six. When you reach these kinds of numbers it is useful to return to the 4 different areas. So now a single person standing here

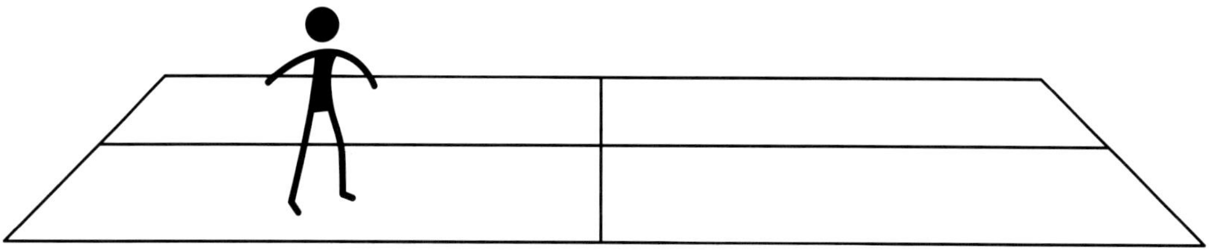

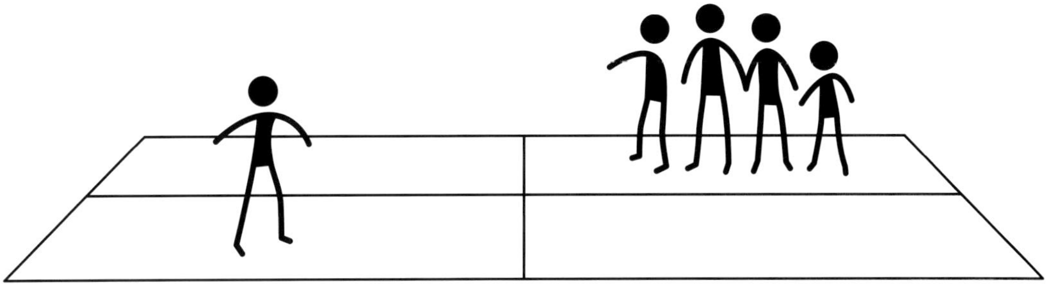

would be balanced by a group here

Point out that a single person above could have the power in the space. The group of 4 could be powerless. On the other hand the positions could be reversed. It is a question of how they impose themselves on the space.

4) Apart from left/right and upstage/downstage space, you can introduce height and depth. The floor to the ceiling and beyond.

5) Look at the flow between people in the space. The dynamic is between them across the space.

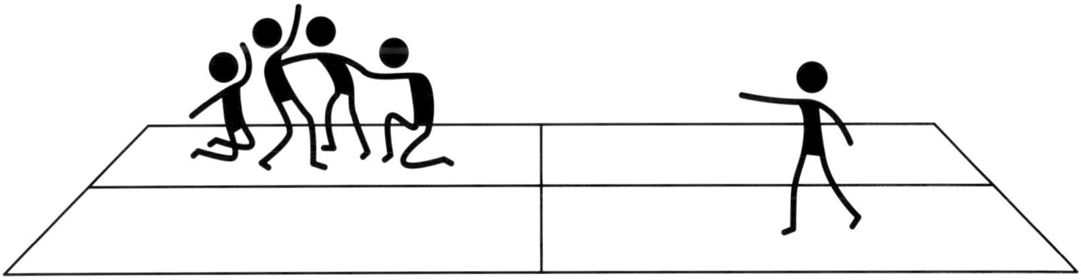

If you step into the frame you can trace an imaginary line in the air from the pointed finger across to the cowering group and link together as one group. Show them imaginary lines from the eyes and the feet.

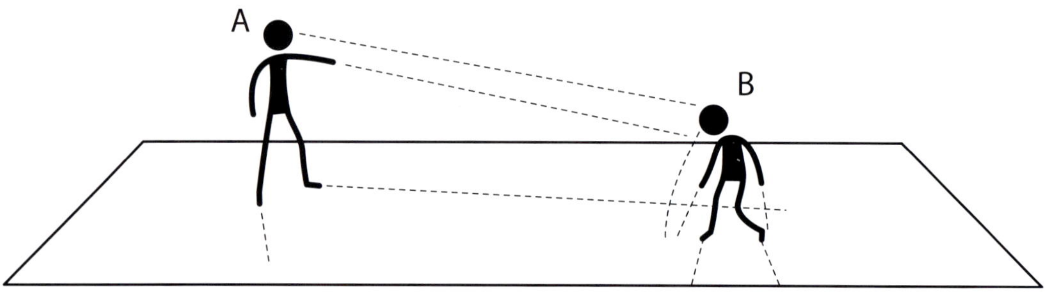

6) Show large art books of paintings with group scenes and an emotional content. Examine the use of space – up, down, left and right but also foreground and background. Notice how the artist makes us look first in one place and then in another, balancing it out with colour and density or sparseness of image.

Ask everyone to close their eyes and open them to look at the picture. Where did they look first and why? What is prominent? What is secondary?

TIP
Get them to solve problems by doing rather than talking

7) Have your pupils work in groups to create a still picture using their bodies as frozen statues in the space. Choose a familiar subject matter such as the Nativity. Give them some time to decide where to place Mary and Joseph, the shepherds, the wise men, the animals and the angels? Who or what will represent the baby Jesus?

Take each group in turn and indicate the imaginary lines running through the space between eyes, fingers and bodies; whether a figure is enclosed unto itself or connected to the next person or echoed or juxtaposed somewhere else in the space. Later invite them to take turns and walk through the picture to comment on what they see.

It is likely that the images they create will be built around the centre of the space with celestial figures higher and Mary and Joseph grouped around the middle, wise men on one side and shepherds on the other and some way off. To some extent they will do this because this scene has been depicted so many times in western art that it has become a cliché.

Point out how they have chosen to use the space. What is used and what has been left. How the characters relate to each other even if they are detached and seemingly separated? Give voice to what you might think a character may be thinking. This is sometimes a revelation to a class as they realise that there is a lot more meaning than they were aware of. It is chastening to learn that your hand hurts when you have to hold your position and that the total picture can have a powerful impact on the observer.

8) Ask them to create another picture; perhaps the Crucifixion, also familiar in western art. Challenge them to surprise you with an unexpected slant on the subject matter. If the Nativity was symmetrical and suggested harmony and order, then perhaps asymmetry could suggest disorder and chaos. It is a question of interpretation of a point of view and an emotional standpoint.

Again it will be difficult for them to accomplish this without talking and agreeing about how they represent it. They discover that you have to accommodate other people's ideas. Again the easiest way to start is to move into the space with an idea.

Whole Group Exercise with Space

Begin with the whole group sitting outside the rectangle looking at the empty space. Give a title, say "Famine." Whoever enters the space first creates an image that suggests the title. The second person has to balance the space and has two choices of action. They can add to the picture created by the first person, near or far but connected in some way, or they can choose to enter another part of the space and create an image that comes from the same title as a new and different idea. Gradually many other people come into the picture until you have a canvas that communicates its theme through the use of space. The composition of the picture is collective and often the simplest image is the most effective.

By stepping in and out of the frame they appreciate the difference between watching and participating. It is easy to see the big picture when you stand outside and harder when you are in the big picture.

7 Deadly Sins

- Pride – excessive belief in one's own abilities.
- Envy – desire for others' traits, status, abilities or situation.
- Gluttony – desire to consume more than you need.
- Lust – craving for the pleasures of the body.
- Anger – losing control and opting for fury.
- Greed – desire for material wealth or gain, ignoring the realm of the spiritual.
- Sloth – avoiding physical or spiritual work.

7 Opposite Virtues

- Humility (against pride)

- Kindness (against envy)
- Abstinence (against gluttony)
- Love (against lust)
- Patience (against anger)
- Generosity (against greed)
- Diligence (against sloth)

Large-scale pictures for different age groups

- A new school
- War
- Holidays

We are all Connected

Have everyone secretly choose two people and on "Go" move so that they are equidistant from both of them (this could be in a straight line or a triangle) they will discover that adjusting for position could be endless because everyone's movement affects everyone else. We are all part of a chain.

Encourage collective use of the space. Those at the back use their upper bodies and hands. Those at the front crouch or kneel. Introduce focus – how everyone relates to a single thing that happens. Create complex scenes where a large crowd of people turn to one person. Make movements and gestures subtle.

For instance create an "unseen" collective chorus who follow 2 people into a haunted house and react with mounting horror as the two characters discover unexpected things (there could be on-looking ghosts moving as one; all the time staying connected with peripheral vision).

CORE SKILLS - TIME

Use different tempos to vary atmosphere.

Examples

- Time is slow - residents in a senior citizens' home talk about their life.
- Time is speeding up - a group of soldiers have to defuse a time bomb.
- Time is slowing down - hearing some bad news.
- Time is fast moving – a fire causes everyone to leave the house.
- Time is fast and slow – escaping prisoners have to get past a guard.
- You fast/everyone else slow – you are in a hurry but the post office queue is slow.
- You slow/everyone else fast – a press conference where you are trying to withhold information.

Varying the tempo increases the tension and mood and makes the work more interesting. This will be useful in production work.

CORE SKILLS - ATTITUDE

By attitude we mean the characterisation/feeling/conflict/tension or mood they bring to the material they are working with.

To create strong attitudes sharpen the conflicts between the characters. Ask your performers to make their situations or scenes have an attitude that is HOT or COLD – not warm. The scene has to be very important to them or their character, not mildly interesting.

Attitude also brings a point of view into the work. At first when you create stories they are simply that – the events of the story. As you get more skilful in your storytelling you realise that the tone of the story, your approach to it, can be constructed in different ways allowing a point of view to emerge. This list by Robert Plutchik (Wheel of Emotions, 1980) was mentioned on page **30**.

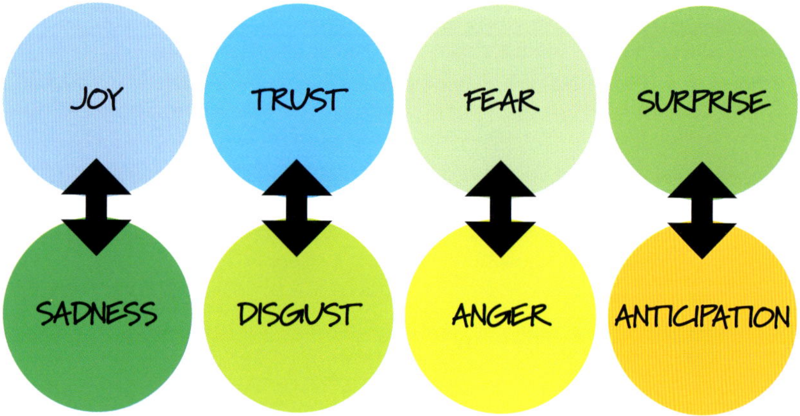

A scientist might measure human emotions and categorise them. An actor finds how the feelings and emotions of their character comes from their life.

Emotions can be explored in role and altered in a scene. By taking opposite emotional states you can create scenes that cause a strong dynamic between the characters. Set up the given circumstances carefully and talk about the degree of feeling in the scene.

1) **Joy** **Sadness**

A is a friend of B. A persuades B to look after their pet while they are away on holiday. While A is away the pet dies. On their return B has to explain to A what has happened.

Tackle it in three scenes or the final events.

The joy of A arriving home and looking forward to being reunited with their pet, tempered by the sadness of the discovery of what B tells them has happened. Some pupils may be unwilling to express sadness. Also you might expect that B would have empathy for A's situation but they might be unsympathetic and greet them with the words, "Your pet's dead." What would be a more challenging emotion to try?

The feeling that A has for their pet is important here.

2) **Trust** **Disgust**

A and B are friends who tell each other their secrets. B begins to say things about a person they both know. It is clear that B cannot bear this person and says things that are rude about their appearance, their family, their house and their mannerisms. A likes this person and becomes disgusted as they listen to more and more horrible things being said about them.

Talk about a sliding scale of 1 to 10 when dealing with degrees of feelings. In this situation one of the characters may make their feelings register at 10 (very powerful) but the other may only be dealing with level 2 or 3. Avoid scenes where everyone plays the strength of feeling at 2; indifference meeting indifference is dull to watch.

3) **Fear** **Anger**

In Victorian times A is the cruel schoolteacher Wackford Squeers in Nicholas Nickleby. He is beating a small child. B is Nicholas, a young schoolmaster who cannot bear to keep silent any longer and who intervenes to stop the cruelty.

Anger can take many forms including anger, rage, outrage, fury, wrath, hostility, ferocity, bitterness, hate, scorn, spite, vengefulness, dislike, resentment.

Here again it would be interesting to see Nicholas' anger growing inside him – made all the more interesting as he knows that if he intervenes it will be the end of his job and bring serious problems with his employer.

You can also play with idea of anger and fear in other ways, for instance the beating of the child can be performed symbolically in slow motion or as a stage fight or by using a chair as the child.

4) **Surprise** **Anticipation**

A is a wealthy parent who returns home with the bad news that they have lost their job and potentially their lifestyle. B is a teenager who is expecting a pony from their parent.

The turning point of any scene often hinges on a moment. It can be very powerful to have a moment of silence or a pause, where one person gradually or suddenly realises that things may never be the same again.

It may be useful to explore the change in movement as well. An emotional event will often cause a physical change in the body. If B is uncaring about the catastrophe that has befallen their parent it may take some time for them to grasp the changed circumstances of their life. The dynamic between these two people is what decides the change. It depends on their character and how they were in the past.

Small group work exploring emotions and feelings

Each situation is a spontaneous task for a group. When they have finished, the rest of the group identify the emotions and feelings. If they are unable to identify the feeling then ask the group to continue making the feeling even more obvious. Props can help these scenes.

1) Anticipation and Joy leading to feeling of Optimism
The group is reaching the summit of a mountain. It has been a difficult scramble but thinking of making it to the top is keeping them going as they imagine what it will be like. Eventually they arrive and the view in every direction is spectacular. This fills them with joy as they ponder on what they have achieved. As a result of this their mood becomes more and more optimistic as they realise that any obstacle in their lives can be overcome if they find a way.

2) Joy and Trust leading to a feeling of Love
A group of soldiers have reached the final day of their training. They have faced many difficult challenges but it time to celebrate what they have achieved. The scene begins with the sergeant congratulating and shaking the hands of every recruit and handing them the treasured badge of the regiment. There is mounting joy and pride in the unit as each person is praised. Finally the sergeant gives a short speech saying that they are now members of a famous regiment, that each person can rely on their comrades. This is the way of the army – a common purpose, pride, honours in battle and teamwork, trusting each other. Instead of wild celebrations this brings about a profound silence as every soldier contemplates what they feel about their colleagues and their regiment.

3) Trust and Fear leading to a feeling of Submission
A bank has a busy day. There is a queue for the tills and a manager is helping the staff. The staff and customers are friendly and open. A stranger suddenly brandishes a pistol. The customers and bank staff are scared and do not know what to do. The robber tells everyone to stand in a group and makes the manager fill a bag with money. The manager complies and asks everyone to do as the gunman says. The gunman makes for the door but before they exit they turn and tell everyone to kneel on the floor. They wait until everyone, including the manager has done so before exiting.

4) Fear and Surprise leading to a feeling of Awe
Some friends are deep in a forest silently stalking strange sounds and lights which have been occurring recently. They are understandably scared. Suddenly a bright light appears overhead and a large spacecraft descends and lands in a clearing. A door opens and to their surprise a large shape stands before them. It is not human. They realise that they are in the presence of a species superior to their own.

5) Surprise and Sadness leading to a feeling of Disappointment
A group of friends enter the school to receive their examination results. A teacher hands them an envelope each containing the information. They open their envelopes and to their surprise everyone has poor marks. This news makes them sad as it has killed off their plans for further education. Gradually their sadness

moves to the bitterness of disappointment at their frustrated dreams.

6) Sadness and Disgust leading to a feeling of Remorse
A group of friends played a game of dares. Stupidly they dared their friend to climb a pylon. The friend climbed up but stretched too far and was electrocuted before falling to their death. This scene takes place at the hospital. It gradually dawns on them that they will never see their friend again and that their lives are changed forever. They blame themselves as they can't rid themselves of the loss they have caused.

7) Disgust and Anger leading to a feeling of Contempt
A group of friends have to deal with someone who bullies a younger child. They are disgusted that anyone would pick on someone unable to stand up for themselves. They stop the bully and the child runs away. The bully becomes a coward and tries to wriggle out of the situation by blaming someone else. This makes the friends angry until they become so incensed that they cannot look at or speak to the bully.

8) Anger and Anticipation leading to a feeling of Aggressiveness
Some friends are talking together. Suddenly one of them begins insulting someone they know. The person who is being insulted enters and overhears the conversation. They are angry at what they hear.

Simpler scenes for pupils aged 9-12

1) Joy
Supporters are watching the national team play in the final of the World Cup. It is the closing minutes and the score is 0-0. Suddenly a player charges up the pitch and scores a goal. Shortly after, the final whistle goes and they have won.

A good group will be able to improvise this without help. It may take a while for them to realise that they have to imagine the game and what happens. Be prepared for a noisy reaction.

2) Anger
The same situation but the opposing team scores.
What kinds of anger are there?

3) Fear
A group of friends are camping together. They are settling down to sleep when a strange noise is heard. They creep towards the opening of the tent to look out

and they see something frightening. Be ready to end this one quickly.

4) Adoration
One of the group is a famous pop star and waits outside the room. Everyone else is a fan who has followed this star for years and now they have the chance to meet them. The pop star enters with their minder.

SECONDARY SKILLS - SOUND

Using Sound and Music as part of your Work
Recorded music can play an important part in your work. Collect music of emotional content in all styles; classical, rock, opera, ballet, pop, electronic, folk – whatever. Add some contemporary music that your pupils will recognise. Film music has a particular resonance as it was written to accompany drama. The music of John Williams, Ennio Morricone and Craig Armstrong are good examples. Choose a wide range of stirring feelings and actions; for instance, sad, quirky, deeply emotional, happy, processional, scary, patriotic. Appendix D has a simple starter list.

TIP
Sometimes the lyrics of a song will add another layer of meaning.

Music helps you create a deeper level to scenes – use it to embroider what is happening. Play it when words are no longer appropriate and feelings take over. How and when you introduce it is a question of taste and experience. Be sparing at first as you can overdo it but have it ready for use at any time. Be sensitive to the new mood you are creating. Something very sentimental such as Nat King Cole's "Unforgettable" would induce laughter at a moment of high drama but if the moment is well chosen it could also introduce a level of commentary and irony in a scene. Some of your music will contain lyrics which add another meaning to a scene.

Many people carry an iPod and portable dock. However 20-30 CDs in a folder can also be useful as they are quick to locate when you are considering several options at once and one is needed immediately.

Use music surreptitiously by adding it to an improvisation to underline the pathos or tension that is being created. This subtle intervention can unexpectedly deepen an improvisation. If you use music as a normal part of your work they will accept it as your repertoire as their teacher. You can also ask them to repeat a scene without words making a new atmosphere with the right piece of music.

You may be surprised how often a piece of music will add to the poignancy of a scene by underscoring a level of emotion that was not apparent to the performers. The music will act as a reminder that underneath the surface of our conversation is a level of emotional feeling that is deeper and more revealing. This introduces the idea of subtext.

As you become more adept at selecting the right music to draw upon, you can become subtle or ironic in the way you play the music against the scene. It reminds pupils that moments of theatre are not only created by words – that the world of feelings is accessed by movement and music. You could intersperse dialogue with scenes that use music but no words.

Create a play to a piece of music. There is a mini project described below. This skill will help your pupils in the second half of the year when they have to prepare longer projects, often using music as a background.

Voice

Use vocal exercises and tongue twisters to focus on developing a voice that travels, with diction. Teach the stage whisper (a shouted whisper) as well as chants and sounds connected to movements. These activities develop the sense of an ensemble and are fun to do as part of warm-ups. Try inventing a radio play by having them perform to the class with their eyes shut or by asking the performers to be outside an open door. Were they believable? What did it do to the story and characters if you could not see them? Encourage your pupils to invent radio plays at home or with their friends. Some phones have a dictaphone element for recording and there are apps for computers that include a microphone. As a stimulus for creating radio plays you could prepare some sound effects to create a mood to work to.

Talk is cheap and you may find that your pupils do too much – allowing their voice to do all the work in a scene. Encourage them to link the movement to the voice of character. Force them to use words of one syllable or invented language or merely sounds in a scene. Explain that communication is more than the dialogue – it should connect with the character's desire and how they feel. If 55% of what we say is conveyed through body language then the words, the tone of the voice and gestures are interrelated.

Encourage them to fill the room with the sound of their voices – collectively and at times alone. If you can make noise together you can also make silence together – an intensive silence after so much noise. This juxtaposition of sound and silence is another controllable dimension.

Explain how effective a pause can be in a scene. A pause is not a gap to draw attention to the next thing they say; it is a moment where their character is unable to speak. Maybe they are deciding something, or surprised by what they have just heard or overcome by emotion. An effective pause has a subtext. The character is thinking – so the actor has to justify the silence or it will seem indulgent. One way to teach this is to ask them to voice their thoughts, or get another member of the group to do it, or even do it yourself. It can be transformational for them to realise that they can think and imagine in character as well as speaking the lines.

SECONDARY SKILLS - MOVEMENT

Using Movement and Physicality

We move and speak automatically in life but it helps to isolate movement for closer study. Often you will meet pupils whose body language is closed. Limbs crossed and weight unevenly distributed. Over time get them to change their posture until they feel at ease in the space. Teach them how to stand in a neutral position. Relaxed, straight, arms by their sides, chin up, feet apart. Then as a group in different parts of the stage space get them to create movement for different emotions. Return to neutral. Young Russian actors learn rigorous mental and physical exercises; it is like basic training in the army.

Rudolph Laban created a vocabulary of human movement. It is straightforward to understand and through it pupils can extend their range of movement and observation. It is not academic and can be felt by the pupil. When you analyse movement you realise that human movement, indeed each part of nature, is circular. Each movement makes a circle or arc between different muscles and joints.

We are built symmetrically with most of our power coming from our abdomen and legs. We are freer with our limbs when moving symmetrically and restricted when we cross our limbs. We are capable of movement up and down, forward and back and sideways left and right. These different movements connect with three qualities.

- Time – how we move – whether it is continuous and slow or sudden and fast.
- Direction – free and flexible or bound and restricted – often expressed as direct or indirect.
- Weight – the strength contained in a movement from powerful to light.

These 3 elements combined with flow gave rise to 8 efforts which Laban created by combining time, direction, weight and emotion.

• Pressing	strong	direct	sustained	think pushing a car.
• Slashing	strong	indirect	sudden	think swashbuckling.
• Floating	light	indirect	sustained	think tentacles undersea
• Dabbing	light	direct	sudden	think typing
• Wringing	strong	indirect	sustained	think twisting wet towels
• Thrusting	strong	direct	sudden	think punching/kicking
• Gliding	light	direct	sustained	think skating
• Flicking	light	indirect	sudden	think twitching

Opposite efforts would be:
Floating and thrusting
Gliding and slashing
Dabbing and wringing
Flicking and pressing

Remember these actions are for the whole body. Create improvisations that incorporate physical efforts in a character. They are cartoon-like and surreal and take people out of their comfort zone.

Some simple Ideas for Scenes Using Laban Elements

1) Pressing and Floating **Police Officer/Drunk**

A scene between a pressing police officer and a floating drunk. The Police officer is direct and makes strong eye contact at all times. They can be close or far away from the drunk but expect respect. They move slowly as they have authority and may lose it if they move too quickly. They also move with strength and certainty. Their voice is commanding but is never rushed, slow and precise.

The drunk moves lightly in all directions (including floor level). They are also slow but they never make eye contact as they are indirect and flexible.

When they have finished keep the same roles but reverse the efforts so that a floating and seemingly out of control police officer fails to confront a commanding drunk.

2) Slashing and Dabbing **Motorist/Traffic Warden**

A scene between an angry motorist and a punctilious traffic warden. The motorist fizzes and keeps losing control of their whole body from the tip of their toes to the top of their head – they explode quickly, powerfully and flexibly in all directions like milk going over on a stove. They can't keep it up forever so each angry episode ends with a pause while they gather their breath and are off again.

The warden is one of those people who know how things ought to be and will not be beaten. They may constantly repeat a movement such as licking a pencil or pushing their glasses up. The lightness, directness and fast speed are constant and precise.

As an encore reverse it and watch a precise motorist and an exploding traffic warden.

3) Wringing and Gliding **Parent/Child**

A wringing child who needs to borrow some money from their gliding parent in order to buy something they want. The need is so strong that their whole body twists powerfully and slowly in all directions, even writhing on the floor with great strength.

Meanwhile the parent moves slowly and effortlessly, lightly with economy of movement, delivered in straight lines.

For a reprise you have a particularly childish and badly put-upon parent who slowly explodes with indirect power while the child is serene and above it all, moving gracefully and elegantly around the room.

4) Thrusting and Flicking **Teacher/Pupil**

The thrusting teacher is direct, fast and demanding last night's homework. Every move, every word is like a punch or a kick in the direction of the pupil. Meanwhile the indirect panicky pupil is like a demented chicken, moving the hands, the fingers, the hair like a twitchy person attacked by a wasp – totally flummoxed.

For the encore an inexperienced twitchy teacher meets a fierce direct pupil who has no intention of giving in their homework and who thinks, "What are you going to do about it?"

It is hard to sustain these efforts for any length of time but it is fun for an actor to try and suck the other into their frame of reference - to infect them with their movement. Who will win?

All of us feel less comfortable with some of these movements. As it is with status we stay with what is familiar to us; all the more reason to be empowered by widening our range. Later in class you can side coach by saying things like "Lighter!" "More direct!" "More indirect!" " Slower!" "Faster!" This vocabulary is a simple way of developing physicality in character work.

TIP
Encouraging exaggeration will develop a wider range of movement

Do

- Make them repeat scenes without words; getting them to convey thoughts and feelings through looks, gestures and physical interaction.
- Play games that encourage them to use the space. Often they neglect the corners or huddle in the middle. Get them to fill empty space.
- Make entering and leaving the space part of movement work. Have a group of people entering quickly or leaving suddenly. Have them invent a reason. Do the same with an exit.
- Ask specific questions. Where are you? What are you doing? Why?
- Work on exercises that get them to occupy the space as a group (equidistant straight lines and curves, letters of the alphabet).
- Encourage your pupils to observe how people move, whether they lead from the head, the shoulders, the abdomen or the hips. Do they move briskly or leisurely in time? Is it a strong or light movement?
- Ask the group to start at one side of the room and walk slowly and menacingly towards you so that you gradually back away and feel intimidated as they slowly close in. The class will love your disquiet.
- Out of class they can walk behind people at a discreet distance and become them by copying their movements. (It may be wise to warn them about the dangers of being discovered.)
- A good book for understanding Laban is "Laban for All" by Jean Newlove and John Dalby.

Learning to observe and embody should be part of the work of older pupils

Replicating Movement
In groups of three ask the first person to walk around the room with their normal walking style. Then ask the second person to join in behind the first copying their way of moving. When they have struck a rhythm ask the third person to walk behind the second exaggerating what they see. The first person drops out and sees the result. No one is made to feel foolish as everyone is working and they are busy concentrating on their own task.

FURTHER SKILLS

Working with a Script

Many pupils are uncomfortable reading from a script. They find it hard to be natural and fluid. A good way to lessen this problem is to work with the whole group on a script where everyone can have one or two lines and where enthusiastic people can have more to do. It becomes a shared experience to make the scene come to life.

Mini Project 1: Emily Wilding Davidson

This scene is for older pupils. It deals with the story of the suffragette Emily Wilding Davidson who was killed when she threw herself in front of the King's horse in the 1913 Derby. The script deals with her background, attitudes, attitudes of others towards her, imprisonment, forced feeding and the pressure to do something for the cause of Votes for Women. There is also a piece of narration (tricky words included) that describes what happened next.

This is an opportunity for you to create a world of words and images that could be claustrophobic but also freeing, one person against the rest of the group – total theatre. A lot of it is in the subconscious and lends itself to abstract images but it often jolts back to reality. You could find an exciting form for this scene incorporating singing, movement and music.

THE DEATH OF EMILY WILDING DAVIDSON

To the sound of humming Emily is thrust into the middle of a large semi circle

Voice: We need you for the cause.
Voices:
Dear Emily's gained a first at Oxford,
She's too clever for her own good.
Why do you stay indoors all the time Emily?
You're going to have trouble with that one Mrs Davidson.
Emily, why are you so bitter?
She always was the odd one out.
Don't play with fire Emily,
Emily you read too much,
You'll never get a husband,
Don't you ever want to get married?
Emily's going to be an old maid.
Mr Davidson, what is your daughter thinking of?
Emily Wilding Davidson today set fire to a post box in Parliament Square causing great damage.
She tried to blow up Lloyd George's house.
Well she had courage.
She must have been mad.
Whatever will she do next?
Voices:
Eat!
Steel or wooden gag?
Force the tube down.
Don't struggle.
The woman in cell 14 has barricaded herself in again.
Turn the fire hose on her.
OPEN!
Hold her head.
Stop wriggling.
Hold her!
Oh my God she's fainted.
She looks very white.
Take her pulse.
Test her heart.
Slap her face.
We've brought you something you've been dreaming of...
STRAWBERRIES
SWEETMEATS

CHAMPAGNE!
EAT WOMAN!
Here! (*They make a circle and call to her but as she approaches another cries out.*)
Here!
(*Until they are all chanting in time at her.*)
VOICES: She said she heard the call of God.
She died for the cause.
Everybody's talking about it (*chorus repeats the "talking about it"*)
Have you read the New York papers?
Have you read the Sydney papers?
Have you heard what they're saying in Paris?
SILENCE
The cause needs a tragedy.
Chorus: The cause needs a tragedy.
Suddenly we see the crowd from behind at a racecourse, excitedly urging on the horses. Emily walks between them.
VOICES: You can't go out there Miss!
STOP HER!
Emily screams.
Narrator: As the last horse passed Tattenham Corner Emily Wilding Davidson ran onto the course and threw herself in front of the last group of horses which were somewhat bunched. By chance – because it was impossible to pick out the purple, gold and scarlet of the Royal colours and aim at an individual horse, Miss Davidson fell in front of the King's horse, bringing it down and injuring the jockey.
The crowd parts and we see Emily lying centre

Miss Davidson was picked up and the colours of the union were found sewn into her jacket. She was taken to Epsom Cottage Hospital where her injuries were thought to be serious but not mortal. With judicious impartiality King George sent to enquire for the jockey and Queen Mary enquired for Miss Davidson. Miss Davidson died on the Sunday following the Derby. Her body was borne in triumph to Kings Cross with a pageantry which recalled the obsequies of Princes. Thousands of women took part in the cavalcade. At the head of the procession was a standard bearer with a banner on which was embroidered "Greater love hath no man than this, than a man lay down his life for his friend."

The verdict given at the great inquest of the nation on the death of Emily Wilding Davidson read:- "Waiting there in the sun, in that scene, amongst the heedless crowd, she had in her soul the thought, the vision of wronged women. That thought she held to her, that vision she kept before her. Thus inspired she cared so much for freedom that she died for it."

(From "The Petticoat Rebellion" by Gareth Thomas and D Emyr Edwards)

The actor playing Emily does not speak but reacts to what happens around her. You make a journey around the stage for her but also place the other actors as a counterpoint to her rebelliousness – maybe conveying something of the stiff authoritarian Edwardian society. It might be powerful to place the group as a semi circle around her or as a tight controlling formation that moves. The race-goers could turn their backs and watch the race behind the action so that we can see Emily preparing herself to walk in between them. The later narration could be highly dramatic by making everyone ritualise the funeral procession and burial.

Using the Script

You can use this script to teach important technical skills. Hopefully pupils would be able to put the script down fairly quickly if they have only a few lines and are aware of their cues. You will often find that young actors are poor at picking up cues and you will notice that there is a perceptible pause between each line. You can overcome this loss of tempo by clicking your fingers between each line; their task is to come in before you click. It takes time to appreciate how to time the entry of a line and they are likely to over-compensate and speak too soon. In time the lines will flow and add more weight to the pauses which are written into the script.

This is the time to talk about the tempo of scenes. Audiences get restless if there is a meaningless and predictable pause between each line. If you added together all the pauses you could be adding minutes of pointless silence to a play. The pauses would be much more powerful if they came after pacey dialogue.

Using the collective power of the group you can create some interesting atmospheres – the snobbishness of the middle-class family, the expectations of a woman at that time, the brutal reality of imprisonment, the pain and humiliation of forced feeding, the techniques they used to get her to eat, the race course, the funeral. Each one of these has a different atmosphere with its attitudes and voices.

You can also emphasise the important unspoken moment of the scene which could be Emily's decision to sacrifice herself. This is something she has to feel, but if you set up the pressures upon her strongly enough it will grow from her growing sense of injustice and commitment to her cause.

A mini project to a particular piece of music.

- Decide on the subject/theme of the story you will tell.
- Choose a piece of music (maybe 3-4 minutes long) that inspires you, has an emotional content and appeals to your pupils.
- Get to know the music well and examine the structure – one way to do this is to study any lyrics.

- Mark 5 or 6 points in the music that are recognisable moments of change (e.g. verse into chorus or a change of verse or key).
- Structure the main events of the story – the journey – to fit these parts of the song. This will give a shape with a sequence of events that fits the music.
- Create some characters to drive the action of the story.
- Tell the story in the stage space using all the actors in a way that engages them with a strong atmosphere and an exciting progression of events.

Here are some tips that might help you:-

- Choose a significant event.
- Use the element of the unexpected.
- Exploit the three dimensions of the space.
- Give everyone something important to do. Create individual moments where one or two people take the focus for a moment or two. Find several of these small moments.
- Bring strong directorial ideas to the piece to emphasise that you are the leader and have creative ideas.
- Find moments where you can draw on their ideas to make the piece more dramatic. This will also draw them closer to the work ("They used my idea").
- Use conflict as integral to your storytelling. Make sure that there are two sides represented in the story.
- Don't get bogged down in minor details too soon. Sometimes it is best to sketch out the whole picture and then do the more detailed work.
- Create a BIG MOMENT in the story – something that changes everything. Find ways of emphasising this. Let us see that big events cause an impact.
- Heighten the theatricality of the storytelling. Deal with the abstract as well as the real. Make the stage pictures and movement powerful and energised. Raise the stakes for the characters.
- Look for the person who is most engaged and challenge them further.
- Look for the person who is least interested and involve them more fully.
- Build the story around a few protagonists but give everyone else a role that collectively is as important as the central character. They could be thoughts in someone's head, observers – something dramatic. Don't make them bystanders with no value to the scene ("I was there too"). Their presence as witnesses should be intrinsic and their feelings towards the characters powerful, whether positive or negative.
- Use the space and the body language to unify the power of the group so that you reinforce the importance of everyone in the group.
- Be poetic, symbolic or melodramatic.
- Expect boldness with their gestures and voices – and work from the shoulder rather than the wrist!
- Use devices such as props to take them to a world of metaphor and symbolism.

- Look for great precision and focus in what they do – whether it is comic, tragic or dramatic.
- Step away from the process of creation. Let them perform while becoming the audience. Ask yourself: Can I see it? Can I hear it? Can I understand it? Is the theme clear? Is there a strong beginning? Is there a strong ending? By taking something short like this (3-4 minutes) you can create a piece of work that will be useful to draw upon in the future.
- Share this work with another class or your Centre Director.

Stage Fighting

Stage fighting has to be safe. It should be choreographed and the participants work as a team. In a real fight things would happen quickly as adrenalin surges and we try to outwit our opponent with surprise, speed and power. In stage fighting we work from the opposite principle and stay in control at all times. What happens is an illusion made through teamwork and choreography.

There are usually three stages to the fight

- The build-up – a signal that something will happen.
- The fight.
- The aftermath.

The person who receives the punch/slap/kick has to react.

Before starting, pupils should remove glasses or accessories that may get in the way.

TIP
Safety first all times. Work moves slowly until they are confident.

The Pulled Finger

This move is about the reaction.

- A holds their finger out.
- B gently holds it but pretends to be exerting pressure. B responds with a lot of movement imploring A to stop as if they are in great pain. It's all about the reaction.

For the following moves the action is usually played upstage and downstage. If played left and right the moves would be seen by the audience.

The Punch

- A (the attacker) pulls back their right hand and puts their left hand on B's left shoulder. B reacts with some alarm.
- Practice at slow speed. A sends a punch from their right hand to B's left. At the same time they take their left hand from B's shoulder. As the punch reaches their left hand A slaps their hands together to make the sound and immediately reclenches their fist and punches the air past B's shoulder.
- At normal speed the slap sound and punch occur closely together. B then reacts and turns sharply to their right as if the blow has landed on their left cheek
- Try doing more than one. B reels from the first blow, buckles and sways and A lands a second blow following the same procedure.
- Swap roles. This move can be effective if A is upstage and B is downstage so that B has their back to the audience. Then when the punch is thrown, B turns to the audience for their reaction. For extra drama ask B to have a scrunched up Polo mint in their mouth which they can spit out as broken teeth.

The Slap

- A holds their right hand back above their shoulder as an open palm.
- B holds their open and outstretched palm in front of their nose as a defensive gesture. Their other hand can be in mid-air, also outstretched.
- A slaps B's palm. It should make a good sound.
- B reacts by turning sharply to the right and holds their hand to their left cheek.
- Swap over.

Practice this slowly at first until they have mastered the necessary partnership.

A harder move is the backhanded slap followed by the forward slap.

- A holds the back of their right hand up high above their left shoulder.
- B puts both hands near their face but their left hand in front of their nose.

- A slaps B's left palm and B's face turns left and puts their right palm before their nose again.
- A reuses their right hand but this time slaps B's right hand from right to left.
- Swap over.

The Punch to the Nose

These moves must be played with the back or front to the audience.

- A holds their fist in front and close to their face.
- Together to see how far A's reach will extend. B stands outside this range.
- A punches forward but pulls the punch back faster than it goes forward.
- B reacts as if punched in the face.
- Swap over.

Funny Moves

Nose

- A puts B's nose between their index and middle fingers.
- A slaps the back of their own hand.
- B reacts as if they have been punched on the nose.
- Swap over.

Punch Bag

- A rotates their fists around each other in a circular motion.
- B rotates their face from slightly left to right as if they are a punch ball. If they flutter their eyes it looks very funny.

The Uppercut

The uppercut is a blow directed under the jaw which would lift B off the ground.

- A makes a fist with their right hand and holds it back.
- B puts their left hand on their chin and their right hand on their knee as if in defence
- A makes a big circle with it in the air, ending in front of B's chin.
- As A's hand makes a circle, B slaps their hands together and puts their left hand down. Their right hand pushes their jaw up and back.
- Swap over.

Punch to the Stomach.

- A puts their left hand on B's shoulder (who has their head down).
- The circular movement stops before B's stomach.
- B jumps up as if it landed on the stomach and reacts.

Knee to the Chin

- A rests both hands behind B's head and B pulls their head downwards towards A's knee.
- B pushes their hands together to make the same clapping sound and before reaching A's knee pulls their head up sharply.
- A does nothing with their hands and keeps their knee still, B does all the work.
- Swap over.

The Fall

Relax, bend at the knee and let go gently to fall. Particular care should be taken with the head. Once on the ground you can make some floor moves.

The Stomach Kick

- B is curled to one side on the floor.
- A brings a kick in but does not make contact; instead the foot moves back again at twice the speed it went in.
- B reacts by grunting and pushing the back further out as if the kick has pushed them.
- Swap over.

The Hair

- A makes their right hand into a fist and places it gently on B's head.
- B holds the gentle clenched fist in place with a hand and cries out as if their hair is being pulled.
- If they are kneeling on the floor they can pull on A's fist and pull themselves up. It looks as if they have been pulled up by the hair.
- B throws themselves down the room, lets go and falls down, rolling over and over as if in great pain.

Once some basic moves have been established you can create fights by putting some moves together. You can link them simply, as professional wrestlers do, by turning the partner into the right place for the next move. It does not have to be done at speed. It must be safe for both partners and the people around them, and the reactions need time to be noticed. You can also intersperse dialogue.

Masks

There are a number of different types of masks that you can include in your collection.

- Red clown noses

- Simple animal and cartoon masks.
- White neutral masks.
- Character and half masks.

When you begin to use masks it is best to work in groups and have others in the group be an audience. A mirror can be helpful to see the possibilities of movement.

- Encourage a whole-body physicality to match what they see in the mask.
- Encourage sounds but not speech.

In groups, describe a place or situation and have the masks react to what they see.

Many pupils are freed by the mask and their movements become larger than life – often in ways that they would not have found without the mask. Masks seem to bring a persona to life. It is not an actor with a mask stuck on them but a halfway point between themselves and the character that lies in the mask or further inside the wearer.

A group of red-nosed masks may behave like young children and have to be taught how to behave by the teacher. It is releasing to have permission for your

TIP

If you use a mirror invite them to make their face imitate the mask.

mask to be naughty or in control of others. One of the empowering devices of wearing a mask is to see the difference that it makes to the other people wearing a mask around you. You see the mask character rather than the person behind the nose; you inhabit a different universe. Without wearing a nose yourself, take a group of these red-nosed people on a visit to an art gallery or a museum. Include the journey there and back in your story. Not wearing a nose yourself gives you a controlling framework to be part of what happens but also to step back and permit developments.

If you use the white neutral mask, teach the wearers to stand in body neutral position and then to extend their posture from the mask and the shoulders. These masks can seem very poetic, even elegant, and they seem to feel emotions very powerfully. Give instructions for a story, play accompanying music and allow reactions to pass between the characters.

With character masks you need to spend more time at the mirror. Invite them to adapt their own face to that of the mask – to become it. Ask for sounds rather than speech. Laughter, crying, fear, love, rude sounds of all kinds, reactions to each other. Often these masks are cut away under the nose allowing the real mouth to become part of the mask.

If your older pupils are interested in this work there are a number of books that describe in detail how to improvise the characters and situations of the Commedia dell'arte. Here there is a movement style for each stock character, a behavioural pattern and a manner of speaking. There are also gags and Lazzi to incorporate into improvisation. Why not create an entire performance from a Commedia plot?

Make your own masks. If you do not want to build one from plaster of Paris you can incorporate sunglasses or a stocking over the face to see how it affects the performer and extends their range. Even an oval shaped piece of card, a photograph of the right dimensions or a cardboard box with holes for eyes can be attached to the face to create a simple mask. Stage make-up can have a similar effect. It is the change of inner intensity you are looking for in the actor.

A Difficult Exercise for Older Pupils

This is for a confident group who like to be challenged. Tell them that they are ready to do something difficult. Give the instructions. Thereafter watch but do not offer any comment on what happens as you are "not there".

> Everyone is asleep in the space. When the exercise begins they wake up. It is a surprise. They have woken up in a different place to where they went to sleep. They do not know the other people and have never seen them before. They

become aware of the place they are in. The space has no windows, no doors. It is lit with artificial light. Ask them to imagine the walls, floor and ceiling and explain the dimensions of the space. Tell them the floor, walls and ceiling are constructed of white tiles. There is no escape.
After a while water begins to enter the room and the water level gradually rises. The water level rises to the ceiling. Places please. Begin.

This exercise is difficult for several reasons. Firstly the subject matter is distasteful as nobody likes to consider extreme trauma. It requires an unselfish and sensitive way of working; whether they realise it or not, they need to work together. You can't hide in the corner. The ending is not specified.

The main learning area here is that everyone has a different version of the same story in their head. Will they accept or not the stories of others and build on them or will they insist that everyone must follow their story?

You can see this as soon as someone speaks (and there were no instructions as to whether the participants speak or not). They may say "Who are you?" or "How did I get here?" Some people readily respond in a way which is chatty and accepting of the situation while others remain silent, avoid contact or are wary of others.

Eventually they will move from the "How did you get here?" to "How do we get out of here?" Maybe shouting for help or pushing against the "walls". It is quite revealing to see leaders emerge and sometimes disagreeing with each other as a sense of panic is present.

The arrival of the water is a key moment. Sometimes the idea is avoided if they do not persist with the information. If they do accept the entry of the water then it is likely to increase the drama and cause the group to respond as one. They will all have a very different sense of how quickly the water is coming in, where from and how quickly. It is quite likely that the level of the water will not be referred to and this can cause problems. Many people will be looking for a happy ending. None of us likes to consider our own mortality. But this exercise does not allow an easy ending. If the water keeps rising then they either start to swim or they drown!

They may sneak a look to see if you are going to retrieve the anxiety of the situation. Eventually someone will decide to "drown." Some will not want this to happen and will insist on trying to revive the "drowned one" but the actor has already removed themselves from the situation and will just float or lie there. One by one the others reach the same difficult point until only a couple are left. Sometimes you find people who hang on in there and somehow survive (and why not?) and occasionally you find people who really struggle and go through the trauma of running out of breath. Usually it ends after all the noise and panic with a slow, silent, still atmosphere.

You may think this is an inappropriate activity for young people to be contemplating but they usually find it challenging and, in an odd way, enjoyable; a challenge to be overcome. Drama is NOT reality and we can step in or out of it and engage as fully or as slightly as we prefer. So, uniquely, this difficult subject matter is entirely safe.

Talk to the group about what they learnt about themselves and about creating drama in a group, what was difficult and how they coped with it. Could they imagine the walls, the situation and the water?

The piece has difficult overtones because there is a sense of torture or intended cruelty in the situation, but this is not spelt out or given a context. They only have the physical circumstances (which they have to imagine and believe in) and each other to make sense of it and agree with.

A group has to be ready for this kind of challenge. In this exercise you are unable to escape, but you also discover how connected you are to everyone else.

Summary for work in September to January

Drama skills and techniques you have learnt bringing your previous knowledge to your work with the group.

The Group – learning to be an effective member of a group, possibly becoming a leader.

Time, Space and Creativity encouraging their use and realising them in the work.

Storytelling – mainly through improvisation – the skills of creating a character in a situation, leading towards playing an intention and devising ideas, connecting with the annual curriculum.

Sound: music, voice and dialogue

Movement : Work on Laban, non-verbal communication and body language.

Attitude: The point of view – creating mood and atmosphere and incorporating emotions.

PRODUCTION SKILLS

The teaching of process skills ends around February and you move on to production skills. Classes are now called rehearsals and your role is to direct while your pupils are actors. Together you prepare material for an audience. As rehearsals continue you step back further and further from the work so that eventually they are ready to perform without your help. Remember, even at professional level a director is partly a teacher.

The teaching team plans rehearsals so that everything is completed in the available time as there are no additional rehearsals beyond the usual centre timetable. As the schedule unfolds you may find yourself assisting the other teachers in their work. The groups are gradually brought together from about halfway through the rehearsal period and step by step the performance work is owned by the group. Your work with them prepares them for what they have to do on stage but you also encourage them to create some of the ideas for the work. By the end of the rehearsal process you watch and comment through notes rather than intervening as they work.

THE CAST

The group is known as the *cast* and when all three groups are together (and with any other centres in a show) they are the *company*. This terminology helps to signal the different way of working. Rehearsals are scheduled into a term or more of work and these can be listed on the notice-board or given as a call sheet. The cast should be clear about what you do – helping them to create and perform the show – and what they do – learning what they have to do on stage and being creative with their performance.

Work your group in a professional and systematic way. Ask them to do research, learn lines, or moves or songs. Your task is to inspire them with some exciting ideas and weld them into work of performance quality. To help you do this the core values of energy, enthusiasm and commitment are necessary and you will find that leaders become crucial in your success.

It is difficult to make progress without commitment so part of your job is to keep your cast motivated. Once rehearsals have begun, the cast work for each other as much as for themselves. If someone leaves it lets down the whole team. So it is important to bind your cast into the project, to give them an idea of what it will be like and ensure that everyone has something interesting and fun to do in the finished piece.

Remember that children and young people find it hard to imagine what the end result will be like. Your support, drive and encouragement are necessary to keep their belief in the project. Sometimes rehearsals take a dip in the mid stage. The initial excitement wears off and the hard work begins to tell. This is another time to talk about commitment and the challenge and reward ahead of them.

Local and Large-Scale Productions

There are three main types of production that you may find yourself working in.

1) A local production involving your centre and occasionally working with one or two other centres.
2) A large-scale proscenium production with maybe 200 to 400 performers usually in a major regional or West End theatre.
3) A large-scale arena production with maybe 1000 or even up to 4000 performers, usually in a major national venue such as the Royal Albert Hall or the O2 Arena.

Each one of these styles of performance has a different approach with a different relationship to the audience.

Using the Show Bibles

In order to prepare in a professional manner and to ensure that everyone goes in the same direction there are show bibles that all teachers refer to for their work.

These bibles include a running order of the show, a brief that explains what is required of staff and a detailed script. There are specially recorded CDs of the musical material. A typical show will have choir CDs which contain separate harmony parts for each choir, lyrics, as well as further CDs for solo singers and backing tracks for the teachers. All this music has been arranged with the songs in the correct key and the band parts arranged as they will sound in performance. Nothing is left to chance.

There are also CDs for dance and drama teachers and DVDs to assist the teaching of choir moves and the moments when the entire company does the same thing on stage.

It is not the purpose of this book to explain in detail how shows are created but it can be daunting to work on one for the first time. It can feel alienating to be given a complicated set of instructions, measurements, expectations and a script. When you are working with large numbers of young people the work will often create a very enjoyable and special atmosphere, but if you have not experienced it before you may wonder where to start.

In a large-scale production with complex stage arrangements it is not your job to question the material. Like a professional you work with the script you are given. You identify what your group has to do and fill the time and space as professionally as possible.

The set-up meeting will explain the project in detail and answer many of the questions you may have, but the size and scale of how it all appears – especially the paperwork – can worry some teachers. Bear in mind that working on a large scale means that the event is larger than the sum of its parts. The energy and enthusiasm that is released at the final stages as it comes together can be quite surprising. Even though the cumulative effect is enormous, the individual contribution is still important. Everyone has a specific job to do and there is pleasure in fitting it together in the performance space. It is often a surprise for the audience who may not have been expecting the sheer scale and spectacle of the event.

In local shows the contact with the audience is more intimate and gentler and there is more opportunity for individuals to stand out. Both kinds of shows are important to give a variety of performance opportunities. The quality of the performance will depend almost entirely on the quality of your preparation.

TIME

The tempo of a performance is important to its success. The music for Theatretrain performances is usually timed exactly. A primary task of drama and dance teachers is to identify the moments of change at different times in the music and to make these key moments clear to the pupils.

A good length for a local show is two acts of about 45 minutes. Large-scale productions usually have two acts of an hour each. It is better to create a shorter work of quality than a longer piece of lesser quality; length is not a measure of quality in children's theatre.

There are two different aspects of time in your work. One is the timing of the show and how that time is used on stage to make good theatre and engage the audience. The other is the rehearsal time from the first to the last rehearsal and your fulfilment of the schedule from week to week.

SPACE

By using the space effectively and confidently you will add to the performance. You take an empty space and fill it to tell a tale to your audience and hold their attention. If you are highly creative you may produce some moments that will stay in their minds long after the performance.

In rehearsal the dimensions of the performance space are marked out with tape or string. This imposes a discipline to your work and makes your pupils aware of being onstage, offstage and standing by, entering and exiting.

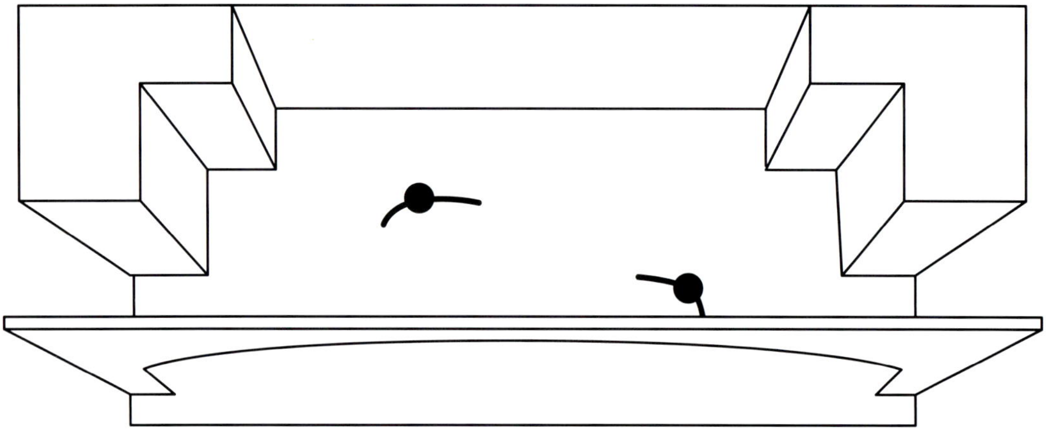

Use the full dimensions of the stage in your work – the breadth, the width and the height of the stage. Consider the sight lines from the audience so that everyone can be seen. You are expected to group people effectively and create focal points for the action. Young people find sight lines a difficult concept to grasp and can unwittingly block the view of others.

CREATIVITY

Use your experience to shape their ideas and make them more theatrical, but allow time and space for them to bring their imagination to the production. The more you use their ideas, the more they will buy into the project. Everyone can be part of this process, whatever their age, and you can do it throughout the rehearsal period.

Young people are often not credited with the wit and intelligence to be creative in this way, but let them make a real contribution and an excitement and energy will follow. It will also test and excite your own artistic skills.

STORYTELLING

The theme is all important. Choose one that has meaning for the cast and the audience. Express it in a sentence that everyone can understand. The theme is not the story or the plot; it is the reason for the story to be told and what we want the audience to think about. For instance *A Midsummer Night's Dream* could be seen as different forms of love.

Large-scale shows have a set theme and storyline. The scenes that your cast work on tell part of a story so one of your first jobs is to introduce to them the whole story by simply acting it out. When they discover the whole story, they are introduced through line of action and they can see how their part fits with everything else. They tell the story with a sense of its conflict, with a variety of means and with changes of mood and atmosphere. They find out which moments are important to emphasise and what is the climax and resolution to the story.

SOUND

Song and speech needs projection. It should grow from the needs of the character or the emotion of the moment. Making the sound big enough to be heard at the back of the theatre takes time and confidence.

MOVEMENT

Movement serves the story through the characters' physical actions. Watching how a group enters and exits tells you a lot about their level of preparation. All movement should be clear and have a variety of tempo and atmosphere. There should be an interesting rhythm between the individual and everyone else in the space, and they should all be seen.

ATTITUDE

Each moment of the story connects to the central conflict that drives the action. This releases a series of different sharp emotions in the work. Creating shared moods and atmospheres that change is an essential part of performance.

THE AUDIENCE

The audience was not part of process work. Now they have to be considered, imagined and performed to. You must decide what you want your audience to feel. You may pretend they are not present or they may be directly addressed. Have strategies ready to imagine an audience in rehearsals. For the younger pupils this could be a teddy bear that sits in a chair. Older pupils may use a large pair of painted eyes on the wall or real people to watch them. Whether you want to surprise, scare or delight the audience, your cast needs to be aware of their connection with their audience.

Finally, they acknowledge the audience's applause. Taking a bow as a group is a skill. Watch performers' faces. Some people do not receive with gratitude. Teach them to accept applause with generosity and pleasure.

Making a Schedule

Establish what you need to achieve by performance day and work back from there. Structure your time to meet targets with the rest of the team.

A simple summary of tasks you must achieve in this period of work:

Preparation

- Study or devise the piece you are working on.

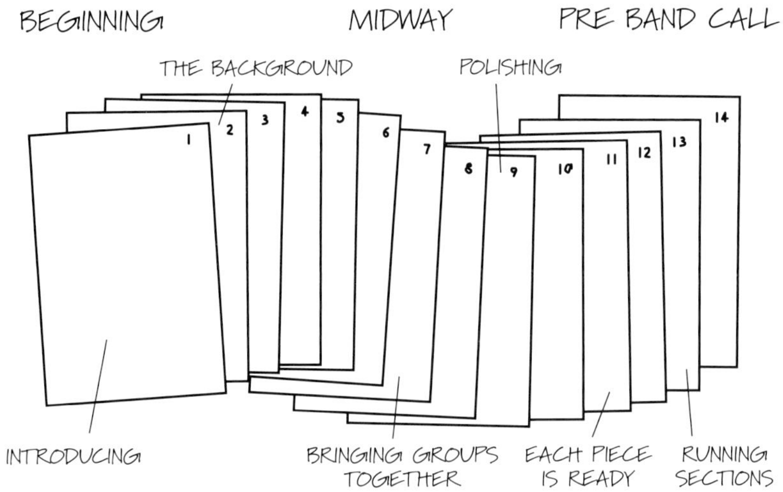

- Ask yourself, why tell this story now? What theatrical style is to be used?
- What do you want the audience to feel?
- Break down the story into simple units of action, each one a separate action often growing out of the previous one.
- Identify the structure and shape of the story such as beginning, middle, climax, ending.

Early Rehearsals

- Rehearsals continue with the three different age groups.
- Introduce a simple synopsis of the story. Make the theme clear.
- Identify the main characters and make the Greek chorus a crucial element of the piece. Give everyone something meaningful to do. Make the circumstances specific.
- Make the conflicts clear and strongly felt.
- Use the dimensions of the stage space in your storytelling; explore entering, the movement about the space, emphasis of key moments, exiting. Can everything that is important be seen by the audience?
- Create a varied tempo to the work. Explore mood and atmosphere.
- Ensure that characters can be heard, that they are clear, and that there is variety of pace and delivery.

Mid Stage Rehearsals

- In large-scale productions the three age groups now work as one.

- Fit sections together and make the shape clear for everyone.
- Use the increased numbers working together to raise the levels of energy, commitment and enthusiasm.
- Use movement and gesture (particularly the Greek chorus) as part of the flow of the storytelling.
- Develop the dynamic of the characters exploring the changing connections:
  - Between each other,
  - Between them and the theme,
  - Between them and the space.
- Make moments of stillness and movement to create variety and a change in atmosphere.
- Investigate the previous life of the characters and help them empathise with their emotions and feelings. Connect these feelings to experiences they have had in their own lives.
- Involve your actors in making some of the creative decisions.
- Use conflict to make the attitudes of all the characters impact upon the audience.
- Identify the moment of change in the story and make this powerful on stage.
- Find a transcendent moment in rehearsals which unifies everyone and makes them excited, sharp and focused when they are rehearsing and performing.
- Ensure that standing by and readiness is part of rehearsals.
- Identify leaders to take the lead onstage to coax a stronger response from all.
- Be ready for the work to take a dip and reenergise the group
- Have a range of strategies to surprise them and keep them alive and excited by the work.

Later Rehearsals

- Investigate more fully the connection between the stage and the audience.
- Look for good habits in the work; focus, concentration.
- Continue to work on what they do offstage and how they enter and exit.
- Gradually step back from the work as they grow in confidence and own the work.
- Rehearse whole sections, make connections and expect variety.
- Stretch the conflict, tempo and atmosphere.
- Step away more by restricting your response to notes after a run-through.
- Polish the weaker moments.
- Invite other people to watch the work and see if they can follow the story.
- Mark them out of ten for their performance. Ask them: “How could we make it better?”
- Introduce costume and props.
- Explain the backstage routine and incorporate this into the work.

- Reach performance level in good time.
- Reread the preparation stage above and see if the tasks are clear in the finished work.

Pre-band Call Week

The whole show is run through in a marked out space, incorporating all; backstage movement as if the audience were present.

Band Call and Show Day

If you have prepared them well your pupils should be excited about Band Call and how their work fits with everyone else. Inevitably mistakes are made and lessons learned. In a large show, learning to fit the different elements together is an important part of the process. It is a good time to invite feedback and to think what needs to be improved for the show day.

The show day has yet more elements to add to the work – lighting and sound are incorporated into the performance, and the building itself with its backstage areas as well as the stage itself will bring a new set of challenges.

After the Performance

Evaluate the performance and the work that led up to it.

Return to process skills and plan ahead for a future performance piece with new challenges.

A Summary

In the second half of the year you guide your pupils to

- Change from classes to rehearsals and teaching to directing.
- Share new performance skills and techniques.
- Focus on the theme of the production through storytelling.
- Incorporate movement, sound and attitude as a natural part of the work.
- Focus on time and space skills as key elements.
- Be aware of the relationship between the stage and the audience.
- Use conflict to give the work a dramatic edge and relate this to movement, sound, space and more particularly attitude, mood and atmosphere.
- Develop theatre skills, new ideas and encourage teamwork.
- Allow pupils to be creative with the work, to bring something of them to it.
- Reflect on the year's work and the progress they have made.

DIRECTING PRODUCTION SKILLS

It is vital that the performers are excited and engaged by the process of rehearsal. The worst approach would be to lay out moves at the first rehearsal and thereafter endlessly polish them until the performance. That would lead to dull sessions where the performers feel they are merely the director's puppets. This approach connects with the discoveries made in process skills earlier in the year. Rehearsals encourage pupils to create some of the ideas and explore the characters and situation through improvisation. For this reason, performance level is built layer by layer during the weeks. This ensures that all aspects are covered and rehearsals are varied and less predictable.

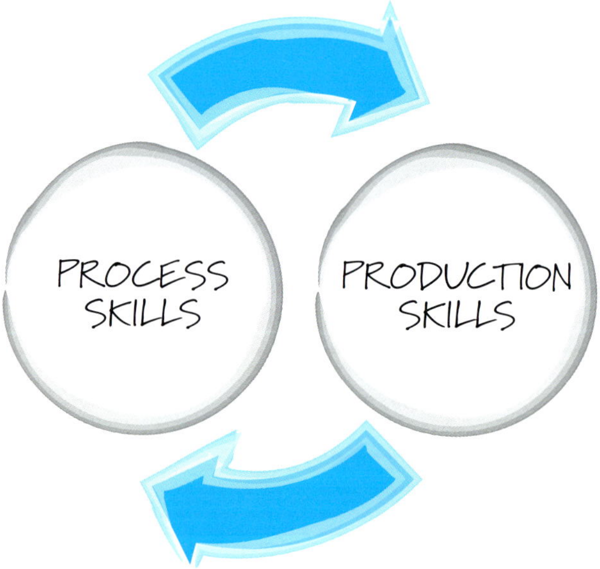

Preparation

If you are creating a local show, then plan it with the rest of your centre team, deciding which elements are focused through drama, dance and singing. Set timings of individual pieces and make achievable targets.

If you are working on a large-scale production you will receive full details of the performance and pieces that you need to create. These accompany specially recorded songs on a CD.

Some questions...

Why this story now?

There should be a strong reason to perform the piece. It should be relevant to the performers and to the audience. You and your cast need to be excited by the story. It is set in a particular time and place, so if you make the story specific for them it will resonate in rehearsal and performance.

What theatrical style will you use? What do you want the audience to feel?

Once you have settled on the story you need to decide what style you are going to use to tell it. This will stretch you and your team's creativity and develop a point of view to the story. How you achieve it will depend upon your theatre experience and how open you are to researching new forms. There are many genres available to you. Some are listed in Appendix A.

Break the story into simple sections

- List the units of actions in the piece. In a large-scale show the actions will already be listed. In a local show you do this.
- There may be about six different points in the story. Each unit usually contains a conflict between two sides or two people.
- Write as simply as possible. Focus on the order of the plot and be aware of the theme that runs through the story.
- Link each event in the narrative to the next. This gives it a through line of action. The sequential events of the plot are significant for the characters. In a good story every scene moves the plot on by giving new information, creating atmosphere and revealing character. Events grow out of previous events and in turn create new events

Identify the structure and shape of the story

Introduction	we meet the characters and discover the background.
Complications	the characters are challenged by problems or obstacles. The characters are tested by events often beyond their control.
Resolution	matters reach a moment of climatic decision.
Conclusion	thereafter things are different.

This shape is familiar to an audience. Not all stories are resolved happily but generally good triumphs over evil and a world of disorder becomes one of harmony. Each story has an arc; as does each scene.

Large-Scale Work

When many centres come together to work there is less emphasis on the spoken word. Large theatre spaces and the number of people involved make

TIP
Collect photographs and pictures as a stimulus to your actors. Encourage them to search for material at home.

that impractical. Instead the work is presented as an amalgam of drama, dance and singing. That means that in a proscenium arch theatre the choir are set at the rear of the stage either side of a live band with a platform in front of the band for use by soloists. The space in front of this, at least 15 feet deep by the full width of the stage, is used for drama or dance. This means that the drama and dance perform actions, while the band and choir sing. Sometimes dialogue is introduced into a performance, but often this is done by using one actor as the voice at the microphone and another actor as the body who mimes to the speaking of the words. This process is a little like the dubbing process used in films.

Your piece may require you to deliver a fully researched piece involving pupils from all age groups telling a story to a four-minute song. The rehearsals described below support that process. In a local show you can use more dialogue in the performance and create devised work as described earlier in this book.

Construct a schedule to keep the work varied and interesting and be ready in time for the performance.

Looking for the Magic Moment

Throughout rehearsals look out for a magic moment that unifies the group in performance. It could be the discovery of a gesture or a look or a move, something that connects the music and brings the company together so much that they can feel a changed atmosphere in the room. If you are lucky enough to find such a moment use it to deepen the work. It can be a game changer for the group and their connection to the work. Everything suddenly clicks into place. It all makes sense and becomes more interesting to them. Enthusiasm, energy and confidence rises and there is a renewed attitude. They want to make it slick, professional, sharp and considered. In a moment you catch a mood which can transfer to every moment of the performance.

How can you encourage this to happen? A lot depends on the characters in your group, their concentration and how the leaders focus on the work. It also depends on your power to make the work theatrical.

When it happens you will feel it. There is a heightened sense of emotion in the room – often accompanied by humour, even hysterical laughter. This release of tension increases the sense of being a company together – an excitement in the shared work. This is the feeling that professional performers work for when they are in creative company. The outpouring of laughter is a sign of shared energy. Can you, as director, find the moment to refocus everyone again?

This is the best of theatre; where actors become so absorbed that they momentarily forget where they are – so deeply are they involved in the work.

EARLY REHEARSALS

Rehearsal 1

Introducing the Project

Aims: To explain the project – enthuse and inspire.

To ask for their commitment through to the performance.

To explain that the process takes weeks and there are new skills to be learnt along the way.

To introduce a simple synopsis of the story.

Seek their Commitment

If your pupils have never participated in a project like this before they may find it hard to imagine. Lay out the scope of the project and explain in a positive way what fun it will be. Touch on the subject matter, talk about the theatre where the performance will be performed and stress the pleasure in being part of a production; the lights, the sound, the band, the costumes, the backstage, the audience and most important their own enjoyment in the work that you are going to create together.

Do

- Talk to them about how the centre has to work as a team.
- Explain that the process of making it work takes many weeks.
- Seek their support. Get their agreement to see the project through to the end even if it gets difficult.
- Tell them that the performance will be more exciting than they believed. Promise to make it fun and involve their ideas in what they do.
- Talk about how everyone supports each other by being there, and about the importance of regular attendance. If someone misses a session then two weeks go by before they rehearse again – a long time to retain information.
- Warn your actors that there is no room for poor attendance – that parts can be taken over by others – and that's fair because the work is what matters.

You want them to create work of quality and work at a high level. The story is new, the group is new and the way of working will give them new theatre skills even if they have been attending classes for many years. Enthuse and inspire and then deliver!

Begin with the story so that they understand what happens and what they are going to do.

Depending on the age group you are working with you could...

- Using the synopsis ask each group to make a dramatic frozen picture for part of the story. Then speak the whole story and have the groups jump up to make their picture at the appropriate moment. This has the advantage of linking the picture to the theatre space.
- Work as a whole class and invite them to make the frozen pictures as you go along – with no preparation. In time they become better at avoiding the obvious and making a more interesting picture. This allows you to work a point of view into their work. Is it realistic? Melodramatic? Humorous? Varied?
- Select people (possibly using the class to self select) to be the major characters throughout and create frozen pictures for each part of the story. The disadvantage of this approach is that it may elevate the importance of some people and downplay the importance of others.
- Using a bag of props, wigs, costumes, etc, improvise the storyline as it is spoken. Here they can mock the story, the characters and situation spontaneously as you speak it. This approach is perhaps best done after one of the above has been completed.

Simple Early Homework

In the early rehearsals it is fun to set a simple homework from week to week. It encourages them to think about what it is happening in the story.

Week 1 – ask them to return the next week with a sentence that describes the story.

Week 2 – a newspaper headline.

Week 3 – a phrase.

Week 4 – a word.

Week 5 – a gesture.

Each week briefly listen to their ideas. Do they really understand what the story is about – the theme? As each week redefines the idea it becomes more difficult. What do they leave in and what do they leave out? To encapsulate things is a useful skill. It is fun to hear them groan when they think they have completed the task and you ask for an even simpler refinement.

At the end of the first rehearsal they should go home excited by the project they are working on and understand the plot. They should feel a strong sense of commitment.

Rehearsals 2-5

Exploring the Characters

Aims: To identify and understand the main characters.

To understand what makes the characters tick and how they are connected.

To create a Greek chorus – making their characters a crucial element of the piece and giving everyone something meaningful to do.

You need some main characters that the audience can identify with and follow on their journey. The characters in stories for children and young people are often good or bad, heroic or evil. This polarisation of character makes the construction of the story straightforward. Balance the actions of the central characters with the rest of the group so that there is a dual focus.

The Greek chorus (this is not a term that you need to introduce to your actors) The actors who are not playing the major characters become the Greek chorus. Collectively the large Greek chorus is another major character. They are present for most if not all of the stage time and play a significant part in witnessing what happens, interjecting at times and reacting as a group to the events as they unfold. The reactions of these characters heightens the dramatic tension of a scene and gives each cast member a sense of importance in what happens.

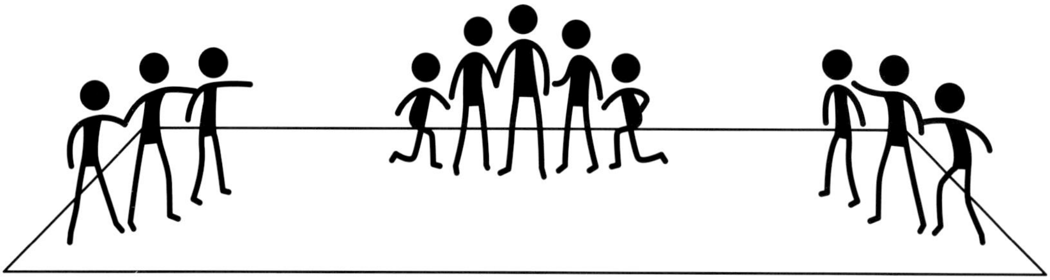

Some Ways to Investigate the Characters

Building upon the work undertaken earlier in the year you can

- Take each major character in turn and explore their behaviour through improvisation. Why do they behave as they do?
- Decide the given circumstances of who, where, what and when?
- Build character history through improvisation – this is described in detail in Chapter 4.
- Discover what each character wants – in as few words as possible.
- Help each cast member build simple information for their character.
- Explore the dynamics and conflicts between the characters.
- Encourage the sourcing of information at home on the internet.
- Ask character questions such as

Passport information. Name. Age. Place of birth. Education, etc

Movement. Are they sudden or sustained, light or strong, direct or indirect?

What happened to them that caused them to be here?

What object might be important to them?

What do they want? A career? Praise? Recognition? Escape? Money?

What is the most important thing their character says or does?

The key question you should ask each of them...

What do you want?

You can start out by saying "What does the character want?" but gradually talk to them as if they are the character. This blending of the character and the actor is fun in rehearsal and makes a more creative atmosphere. Every character should know why they are on the stage. and as the story proceeds their character pursues what they want while dealing with what is happening before them. So you have to find a simple way for them to know that their character wants.

Do

- Keep a check on your rehearsal schedule and its targets.
- Plan wisely so that everyone builds up a picture of their character and their journey. The past, the present and the imagined future.
- As rehearsals proceed, find a moment for everyone. A look or gesture that for a moment makes them the focus of what happens.
- Explore the situation and characters through the imaginations of your actors.
- Excite them with what they have to do.
- Encourage them to explore ideas at home.
- Teach them that their actions are important.

Don't

- Begin your rehearsals by blocking the moves. Begin by investigating their character. Reducing acting to where you stand and what you say is counterproductive to this process.
- Ever have a group of performers sitting around doing nothing. Keep them constantly involved in what you are doing.
- Keep repeating scenes – if you must run a scene again add a new element to it to re-engage the performers' attention.
- Say things like "in the business you have to accept repetition and periods of boredom." They are not in the theatre business and they want excitement, not sitting around waiting for something to happen. Be hyperaware of their interest in the work.

Eventually you will reach a point where the group has understood the plot and the characters and is ready to set it in the space and see how and where the characters move.

MID REHEARSALS
Putting the work together on stage and exploring the dynamics

Rehearsal 6 SPACE

Aims: To group the action on the stage effectively and make sure that everyone is seen.
To explore the relationship between the space, character and status.

This is the first session where you will place the actors in the space. Be decisive. They need to have confidence that you are leading the work. Try out some of the groupings of characters at home by making a scale map of the stage dimensions and using a set of chess pieces to represent the performers.

Some things you should consider:

- The story requires a range of different moves in the space. It is more fun for the actors if they can have varied parts of the space at different parts of the story.
- They need to be seen. How you arrange them in smaller groups will make the story clearer for them and the audience.
- The positions from which the audience will watch the performance.

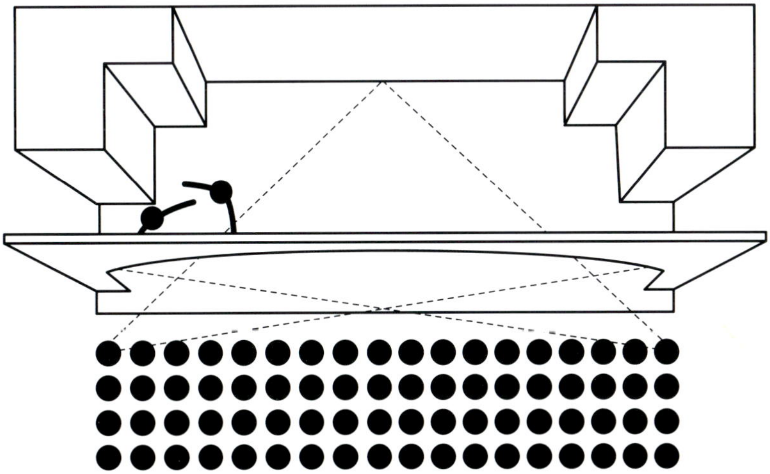

Be aware of these sightlines when you position your cast. Draw a line into the middle of the stage from the furthest seat left and right at the front of the stalls and the circle.

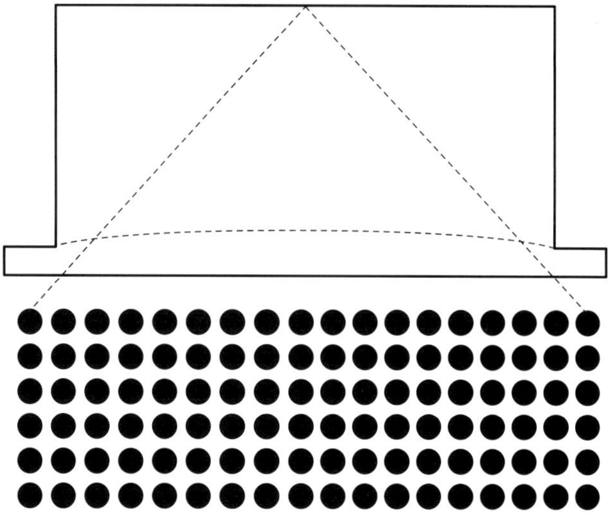

Lay out your chess pieces as the main characters in the story. Then add the Greek chorus into the space surrounding them. Once you have your opening positions you can decide where they move to at the next change of action. Even this early you can consider *how* the moves are made from position to position – tempo, character motivation, attitude.

Some things to consider when using stage space...

- Mark the centre of the stage at the front and ask your actors to use this mark to be in the same place each time. The mark is used at the theatre to help them get their bearings. Marking the centre divides the acting space up into four different spaces (as outlined in process work).
- Use the full width and depth of the stage. Do not leave an empty 'corridor' between the acting area and the audience.
- Use height and depth – from lying on the floor to being lifted high. It adds dramatic impact to the stage picture. Even a chair or bench can introduce a new level.
- Put gaps between the main characters so that you use the whole stage to tell your story. This creates a stronger dynamic between the characters.
- Fit the Greek chorus around the main characters. For example the actors could...

1) Spread throughout the stage at different heights (sitting, kneeling, crouching, standing, hands held high, etc).
2) Lie on the floor in random or organised formations.
3) Curl up tight on the floor.
4) Stand in rows (this works well for military formations, churches, schools, etc).
5) Use two people to stand still and signify a doorway and have everyone else walk between them.
6) Surround a main character with friends, family, supporters, etc. Take care that those standing in front of the main character don't obscure the view of some of the audience. Solve this problem by having those at the front be lower (kneeling, crouching, etc) or by using shorter people in this place. They can even be in front with their back turned to the audience as long as we can see the actor's face.

The audience should know from seeing how the space is used. Do not assume that they will know unless you make it very clear. A large sign or particular props or costume may be necessary information.

If you have several locations in your story you must find a way to show this.

- You could move in double speed or slow motion or an exaggerated/stylised way.
- If the scene is set in the same place throughout then invent reasons for the main characters to move about the stage and for the Greek chorus to follow them.
- Later on these moves will be very precise but for now block them quickly and freely.

TIP
Make some of these decisions with the group, using their ideas.

- Fix where everyone will enter and exit. Decide the exact cue to enter. Are they discovered on? If so they still need a cue to enter.
- Make the final event into a strong stage picture – perhaps a group pose or a final flourish. Bring the situation to a clear conclusion to invite applause.

Entering, moving together, separating, stillness all create strong dynamics.
It can be powerful to have the whole group gathered together in one part of the stage

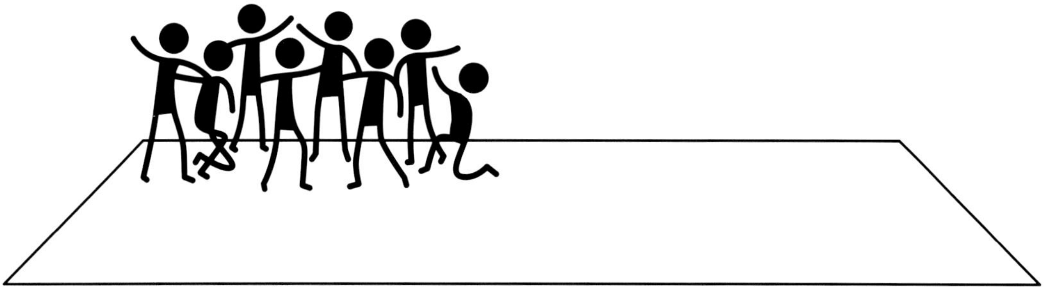

One person versus the rest looks very powerful.

How might the court of a king or queen be arranged to demonstrate their power? How could you create a prison or a ship? A master criminal's lair? A hairdressers' salon?
A busy market? A racecourse?
Imagine how costume and props could help you define the space and the characters that are in it. Props particularly can add a symbolic or ritualistic level of meaning. A sword, a candle, a globe, a doll can all be power metaphors in your story.

Collectively is your group going to make straight lines or curves?

Curved Shapes (coming from nature)
Circle, arc, ellipse, parabola, arch, quadrant, arcade, bow, crescent, half moon, semicircle, horseshoe, loop, and abstract and haphazard shapes.

Straight Shapes (coming from mankind)
Symmetry, right angle, quadrangle, diamond, star, row, triangle, square, rectangle, pentagon, wedge, cube, pyramid shapes set with equidistance and precision.

How can you build status to the stage picture? A powerful ruler like a king or a gang leader would not allow someone to stand immediately next to them. The acknowledgement of their power might extend as far as the edge of the stage. How you place them in the picture will tell us who has the power and how they are respected. When people move they will adjust to the person with that power. In this early session insist that they are in character. They should know why they are there and what they want from those around them.

The Halfway Point of Rehearsals

You have reached the middle of the rehearsal period. When you are working on a large-scale production this is the point where you bring the different age groups together to work as a company. If your previous session on space was straightforward it should now be comparatively easy to slot the three groups together. Inevitably there is a settling down period while everyone learns who they stand next to and who plays what character but the greater numbers will create a new atmosphere which you can use to your advantage.

Some pupils do not like working with other age groups. Be sensitive to this and keep it fun for everyone. Do not allow anyone to sit around and watch – keep everyone busy and creative at all times.

If you get ahead of schedule in the weeks ahead and sense an impatience with working as a large group you could revert to separate classes for a week.

Many problems can be solved by creating sub groups or families to give the Greek chorus an instant connection.

Be watchful over those pupils who prefer working with their own age group – particularly those who may not draw your attention it.

Working in a larger group means that you have an extra teacher working alongside you. You should both know the aim of the rehearsal and what is to be achieved in the time. You are both free to use your creativity to improve the work. Having one teach while the other watches is a waste of useful energy

Rehearsal 7 TIME

Aim: To fit the units of action to specific points in the music.

This week is about completing the journey in the space that you began last week. Then you were laying out the basic outline of what happens; now you are focusing in more detail at particular moments in the music. If you are working on a local show this is where you must tie down the exact length of your piece.

You have probably created about 6 different events in the story. This session will connect each of those events to a precise moment in time. The production notes give exact timings for these events. If you are creating your own piece you can decide these moments yourself or with the group. The music will give you a length and structure that in turn you can break down into smaller sections.

- Introduce the characters and groupings in the story.
- Rehearse each of the changeover moments and determine the tempo of how it happens – quickly or slowly.
- Explain precisely where the change occurs in the music. You can work to a stopwatch or the timer of a CD player or iPod but ask your pupils to listen out and learn change in the music. Each one of these moments is chosen because musically they feel different.
- Return to the structure you laid out last week and make each change happen on cue to the music. Encourage your leaders (possibly the main actors) to take responsibility for moving at the right moment. Thereafter the other actors can take their cue from the leaders and seamlessly new positions should happen on cue.
- Explain why different units happen in different parts of the stage – tell them that the changeover moments will become character-led changes.
- Show your actors how each section of the story causes the next incident – cause and effect. Don't get bogged down in too much detail. In future weeks there will be time to fill the moment-to-moment life with more details but expect it to take you a whole rehearsal with everyone to fit the story to the music.
- Consider using different timescales in your structure. Freeze frame some characters while others continue to move. Incorporate double speed, slow motion or acceleration.

TIP
Make some sudden unifying moments where everyone does the same movement. It can be very powerful.

If you are devising your own story without music use this rehearsal to set the length of the piece and as above set the basic structure in the space. Don't make the piece too long. 5-7 minutes maximum is a good length to keep the audience interested and give your actors enough time to work in detail. If necessary use a kitchen timer in rehearsals to keep to the right length.

By now everyone should now know how the story fits to the music.

Rehearsal 8 SOUND

Aims: Taking sound as your starting point, to fill in the smaller details of the moment-to-moment life.

To direct the audience's attention to the important things that happen.

To give any spoken dialogue your close attention.

For the last couple of weeks you have set out the outline of the work. This was necessary so that everyone could see appreciate the structure. Now there is time for creativity.

The sound of the music has other qualities that can help you. It can express the feelings of the characters and carry their thoughts or make a new atmosphere.

- Make the focus clear so the audience knows where to look and is not distracted by something unnecessary. Talk about levels, 10 being the centre of attention, 3 being unobtrusive.
- Work everyone together. There is no time for people to go off in groups and come back with ideas. Work through from the beginning. Listen to people's ideas and try them out, adding them if possible. The more complex the work becomes the more interesting it is. This is why you need to begin with a simple structure and layer the characters as you go. The later rehearsals will return to simplicity but here the work can be more detailed. Individuals from the Greek chorus can have a moment where they take the focus. Look for a strong engagement with other characters. Stand back, watch what is happening and change the focus as necessary.

TIP
Watch everyone to see if they have a clear reason for being in the scene.

Find particular moments in the music – for example, a precise sound of percussion – and use it to make something prominent. If you search for these moments they will make the work more detailed and fun to perform. You can have the company make sounds during the scene, vocally or physically. They can also join in the singing at particular moments in a sudden and passionate way. Immediate silence and stillness can be equally striking.

At this point in rehearsals it can be useful to run through the piece in silence **without** the music. If they can make sense of the journey then they have understood the preparation. There may be indecision about some moments but if leaders take responsibility for moving things on and they are responsive to each other they will succeed. Unexpected discoveries may appear along the way.

TIP
Don't forget, a pause is usually a moment when the character has to think rather than speak.

If your piece uses speech this is the week to stress the importance of the voice in the theatre.

- Can they be heard?
- Is the diction clear? Encourage the actors to stand further apart and explore how sound and space are interrelated. In extreme cases use opposite ends of the hall to get them to open up their voices without shouting.
- Check that they are breathing properly and deeply before they speak. Look at tone, accent and variety of delivery.
- Make sure that they listen when they speak. Don't let them merely wait for their next line or they will settle into an agreed pattern of how to deliver the lines. Encourage them attend more fully to what others say.
- Make sure that they pick up their cues. If they leave a perceptible pause before speaking each line they will add time to the play and make the audience restless. If this is so look again at the exercise in Process skills on Page 71. A benefit from this would be to give more power to any pause. Too many small pauses cancel out a proper pause but now it would have impact.

Rehearsal 9 MOVEMENT

Aims: To focus on the character's movements both in groups and as individuals.

To giive closer attention to entrances and exits.

To build up the moment-to-moment action of the play through action and reaction.

After the details and new discoveries of last week it is time to look at the journey of all the characters about the stage.

- Begin by reminding the actors of their entrance and exit. In large scale productions there are instructions for the backstage procedure and it is wise to incorporate these from this point in rehearsals. It saves you having to scramble through instructions in the later rehearsals. Although they look complicated most of the backstage instructions can be given in a few minutes and thereafter included whenever you run through the material.
- Expect them to be in character before they cross the line of the stage. Don't let them enter and then assume the movement of the character. Likewise insist they remain in character until they are off. The actor who enters, alive to what is happening, reacts to events and then departs having been even physically altered by what happens, is fascinating to watch. A lot of young people's theatre looks artificially contrived as if they are repeating moves decided upon weeks before and then copied over and over without any spontaneity.
- Entrances are worth spending time on as they are important for the character and set up the scene that follows.
- Insist that the audience understands who these people are, where they are

and what they are doing. Don't underestimate the importance of making a clear set-up. Sometimes the cast and the director can be so close to the action that they assume that what they do is obvious to the audience – often it is not.

- Demand a strong response as you move on to the next section. Encourage confidence by having leaders who are fearless. Make the stakes for the characters high. Make them care about the outcome of what happens.
- Demand a strong vocal delivery. Young actors will often give an underpowered vocal performance that would not be heard by most of the audience. They need to project with more physical and vocal power than they may have imagined. Being in a group allows them to do this with gusto. Play one group off against another.

Experiment with exaggerated movement.

- Divide the company into groups of 6 and have them partner another group of six.
- Group A makes a series of big movements that Group B has to mirror. Then Group A can begin to move around the space as one with Group B following. It is fun to see different groups keeping the exercise going while negotiating with other groups who are trying to pass. You can also give A an emotion from the scene which they can project. Make sure that B also has a turn at leading.
- Divide the group in half and have one be the audience while the other shares a section of their scene. They will learn a lot from watching them adjust to your instructions. They are learning about how big their movements have to be if they are going to be seen from many feet away. An audience prefers confident and imaginative physicality to understated movements.

Move through each of the sections of your story and talk more about the chain of actions, reactions and consequences. Think of a snowball fight. It's a game and part of the game is the unexpected (I'm attacking? I'm defending? Whoops!). On stage it would need structure, a set up and a pay off.

1) "Watch me, I'm going to throw a snowball" (Don't miss this!).
2) "What!" (The hit).
3) "Ouch that hurt!" (The reaction).
4) Look what happened to me!

While 1 is the build up – signalling what is about to happen, then either 2 or 3 can be the bigger moment. It's a choice. The look of horror or a sudden change from a smile to shock can be quick in 2 but perhaps slower in 3. Small children do this when they fall over, instinctively moving from silent shock to surprise, through a trembling lower lip to bawling their eyes out. It is your decision as you work out the connection between each of the events on your play. 4 gives an opportunity for the injured person to be hurt or outraged. Some footballers are particularly good at this.

- Give each unit a mini sequence of events.
- Return to the characters' histories from earlier in the term. Remind the main characters what they want from the people around them and particularly the person they are up against.
- Get them to connect what has happened in the past with what they want to do in the future. Here they are stuck in the *now* but this is not where they want to be! That makes them interesting to us as we wonder what they will do.
- Every time they start the scene again introduce a new element, an adjustment which will cause a different response. This in turn will affect others as they are forced to deal with what is in front of them.

Expressing this in movement spurs their creativity. Stand back and think how you might sharpen the actions and reactions in the scene.

This is detailed work in sections. Don't make constant run-throughs of the piece. Today's emphasis on movement should draw attention to the physicality of the actors in the space, their ever-changing focus, the moments of change and to character and status. If a stranger walked into your rehearsal they should be able to spot the characters' status.

The Greek chorus in their sub groups need to have a physicality in common or it could be highly individual with different styles. Whatever is decided they are part of the stage picture and their collective character will resonate in movement.

As you gave attention to the entrance you should also spend time on the exit. Make it in character and leave an impression. Be creative with the characters in the way they leave the space.

If you are rehearsing a scene with words, this week's emphasis on movement will give you chance to link physicality with the voice. Words affect movement and vice versa. A moment of change in a scene can radically change voice and physicality.

Rehearsal 10 CONFLICT

Aims: To make the conflicts clear and strongly felt.
To understand which side of the conflict they are on.
To build more detail.

A way to engage your company more deeply in the work is to make the conflict between the protagonists as powerful as possible. If there does not appear to be a conflict in a scene then invent one. Ensure that you have two sides represented on the stage. It could be one person against everyone else or two groups in opposition to each other. Everyone is on one side or the other.

If you are working on a scene where one person has all the power then we should see how the other characters acknowledge that power. They know their place. Some may be terrified of him; others may be impressed by his power and want to please him. They do not have the luxury of expressing their feelings in his presence; they have to keep it hidden. This tension between what they feel and how they behave gives more depth to the character.

The more specific you can be, the more interesting this situation can become. Say your characters are working for an international criminal organisation run by a Mr Big. Through improvisation you could explore how they joined, how they were interviewed, what happened on the first day? When was the first time they felt uneasy or when did they decide that they wanted to impress the boss? If the actors improvise these events their work in the scene will have a richer dimension. You might improvise some of them trying to escape or sabotage the work they are doing or they might fear that someone would inform on them. Gradually during the rehearsal period you raise the stakes of the situation.

A sharp conflict between opposing forces makes a story more compelling. As you watch think how you might increase the conflict between one side and the other.

A more obvious conflict could be between social classes; the haves and the have-nots. Your task would be to exaggerate the behaviour of the two types. A difference in body language would create an immediate contradiction. Juxtaposing opposites in scenes causes tension which can be released with humour or aggression.

- Try exploring the conflicts with Group Pictures of the Characters. Take a main character and stand them in the centre of the space. Everyone in the company has to show how their character feels about the character in the middle. This is not a representation of how their character behaves towards them in the play but how they feel inside about them. If they admired them or wanted their attention they might move closer. What position would they take up? Would they stand? Sit? Lie down? Extend a hand towards them? Smile? If they hated them perhaps they would they move further away and express contempt or even turn their back with a hand raised in anger.
- Encourage a committed response but make the feelings sharp. If they choose to be bored make it an extreme form of boredom. They might put one finger against their mouth or die of boredom on the floor. Always provoke a stronger response from what they give you.
- After you have counted aloud to 10 ask them to freeze. Wander around the picture commenting on powerful images and encouraging others.
- Ask some characters to say aloud what they privately think about the person.
- Move onto the next character. If you were working with one age group you would have time to work your way through every character but with a large group it may be better to restrict the pictures to the main characters in the narrative.
- Return to the scene and incorporate these new feelings about the character.

This rehearsal is a time for details. Everyone in the company should have a moment that matters; a gesture or a shared look. If you give that moment or idea a focus it draws them closer to the work and makes them realise that everyone in the scene is important. No one is an extra.

> You may face the problem of pupils who are irregular attendees. You need regular attendance; without it the work of everyone lessens. You can back this up by dropping moments of action if the actor misses one or two weeks. It is better to find a new idea as it is hard to stand in for someone. When they return you might have to say "I'm sorry we had to cut that moment because you weren't here and it was holding everyone else back. We changed it." They can't really complain if they weren't there.

As a director always think how you can get more from them.

- More passion, more connection to what is happening.
- Look out for the work becoming diluted, losing its power or corners being cut. This can happen when you repeat things. There can be a tendency to settle for playing safe and not sustaining intensity.
- Find strategies to maintain a high level of energy.
- Use humour and seriousness, surprise them with a new instruction, even whisper a new instruction to one person to see how everyone responds.

- Keep the work alive and interesting for them. You are the person to make the atmosphere challenging and connected to the story.
- Have a personal connection with every actor and be watchful for what they do at all times.

By the end of the rehearsal everyone should be clear about whose side they are on and how intense is their feeling.

Rehearsal 11 THE BIG MOMENT

Aims: To identify the big moment of change in the story and make this powerful on stage.

Who is showing commitment and energy?

By now the story has shape and movement. There is attention to detail and there are different atmospheres. Most of the important decisions have been taken but in your story there is a big moment. It is usually near the end of the story and brings the conflict to a climax and points to a conclusion. After this moment things are changed forever.

- Decide what action will cause the big moment and how you will make it significant.
- Heighten the what-is-going-to-happen-next feeling.

- Pare down instructions and information to simple things.
- Exaggerate the big moment with a change in tempo, atmosphere, movement and attitude.
- Bring the internal or external conflict to a head.
- Have everyone participate and react.
- Contrast the body language, sound, movement and attitude before and after to emphasise the moment of change. The previous actions in the story and the interaction of the characters have been leading up to this moment.

To emphasise this you might ask, for instance:-

- The characters to be completely still or move in slow motion.
- The focus to be pulled to one place.
- One character to make a gesture.
- A fight to break out.
- Someone to win (and someone to lose).
- A prop to be used significantly
- The sound to change.
- The lighting to change.

Whether the big moment has been profound or flippant there will be a change in the body language and demeanour of all the participants to the event. They are changed by it and we need to see this.

Life moves on. The big moment has passed and the characters have to deal with the consequences. It might be triumphant and joyful, sad and despondent, fearful and scared or loving and happy. They cared deeply about the outcome so whatever new state is reached it should be powerfully realised.

LATER REHEARSALS

Polishing and Completing the Work for the Audience

Rehearsal 12 ATTITUDE

Aims: To look more closely at the different sections of the story and create bigger contrasts throughout.

To encourage a strong personal connection the character.

Last week you focused on a particular moment and made it the most powerful moment in the piece. Now you return to each section of your narrative and make bigger contrasts between the emotions and atmospheres. Use what they discovered last week and spread an intensity of feeling throughout the piece.

By now they should be less inhibited and readier to enter different moods at different parts of the story.

- Make more of the contrasts between characters or groups of characters in different parts of the stage.
- Inexperienced performers tend to pick up a uniformity of performance; surprise them with how much variety they can still make in the piece.
- Describe an action word for each section. Each group can have its own short list of words which can be secret from the others. Make sure that you can see the action that is their word.
- Take the sections apart and make changes of mood apparent through character, status, time, space and particularly the conflict.
- Each section should cause the next to be more deeply felt.

Don't

- Settle for what has already been arrived at.
- Allow your actors to think that the work is completed. In these final stages you need even more focused energy and commitment from them all.

Attitude is the means of bringing the elements of theatre together in the performance. You have been working with feelings for weeks but the purpose here is to underline the huge differences between each of the sections.

If you feel that you need to change the group feeling try:

- Acting out a version of the story that mocks what you are working on. Make it ridiculous. Play it for laughs. Maybe use masks and different music. Change the main characters and use younger pupils as the leading roles. Take the work somewhere else. Give the work breathing space and then come back to it with renewed focus. Allow a last chance to play with the material before things become fixed for performance.
- Explore the atmosphere and mood by performing without music; stretching out the time so that it is longer. Allow the atmosphere to be extended. Make the moods extreme, tempos fast or slow, movement strong and powerful or slight and light, direct straight lines or indirect curves. Emphasis the difference between each mood and the signal to move on to the next mood from yourself or at a cue given by the leaders.

Ask yourself if the style you chose during your preparation is evident in the final result. You still have time to make a change.

This week can also be a good time to incorporate costumes into the work as they can help change the atmosphere, another step closer to performance.

Rehearsal 13 THE AUDIENCE

Aims: To give the play over to the group.
To consider the audience; what you want them to feel and what might be their reaction.
To prepare the backstage organisation.

The time for working on the play has now finished. It is time to step back, consider the audience and to deal with the procedures that happen offstage.

- Run the play. Do not interrupt or help in any way. Be the audience for them. If you have problems then emergency measures may be necessary but you want them to be in charge of what happens.
- Take notes and give feedback – and a small amount of polishing – after they have finished a run-through. Psychologically this is an important moment. The leaders are the people who take on the responsibility for making things happen. They make it happen while you watch. This is a natural part of their preparation. Stepping back also means that you can be more objective about what you see and become the proxy audience for your company.
- Invite in a couple of people to watch. The cast will respond to having an audience, even if it is one person. This person's private reaction is useful to you. Could they follow the story? Did it make sense? What was not so clear? All of these reactions are useful.

Many young people imagine that the audience is automatically interested in them and take their attention for granted. Shock them out of this complacency. Be their audience but don't look at them. Explain that they have to make you interested in watching them and that they have to engage the audience so they find it irresistible to watch. In later rehearsals corners get cut because young actors often think "This is easy; we know what we are doing." They stop going through the thought processes. It might surprise them to know that you can see this in their performance and that you don't believe in what you are watching. Being a surrogate critical audience is a useful tool for encouraging them. For fun you could try yawning loudly or laugh appropriately as you watch and see if they can deal with it.

You may be working in a genre that directly addresses the audience or involves them in the action. Audiences like to be involved and comic scenes can have interplay of laughter between the stage and the audience. Are they ready for the unexpected reaction? Try laughing in the wrong place.

Return to the first question that you asked yourself at the beginning of this process. What do we want the audience to feel? How are they to be changed by what they see ? Will you put a spell on them? Will the work be memorable at the end of the evening or even the next day? The best performances are remembered for a long time.

At the end of the evening they have to leave the stage and acknowledge the applause. Audiences like to see a reaction to their applause. It is gracious to accept it as a gift. Find a suitable acknowledgement to the applause – it's all part of the theatre experience.

In large-scale productions your cast is working with many other groups. The coordination of entering, exiting and moving backstage should be smooth and fluid. The backstage notes have already been part of your final rehearsals. This week practise what has to be done before and after their time on stage. There are set areas backstage to get used to. Prepare your leaders separately and have them organise the backstage journey. If you are using chaperones with the group bring them into rehearsals and give them a copy of the backstage notes. It is not something that they can suddenly understand at the theatre – they need time to appreciate how it comes together.

Rehearsal 14 PRE BAND CALL RUN THROUGH

Aims: To prepare the company for next week's Band Call.
To polish sections that require it.

In large-scale productions the band call is the first time that all the performers come together. It is a run-through of the show often using a live band and amplification and a marked-out stage. This is where the backstage notes are tried out with the other performers. Now you can see your company working under pressure. They are watched by hundreds of other people and in turn they watch others. It could be intimidating and competitive unless all the performers were taught to respect each other. They have to become a team who work for each other and respect each other. This means that they are silent backstage for other performers as they expect them to be in return.

The entire show is run through in order. This involves them singing, dancing and acting as well as moving around thc room as at the theatre. As the work is completed the emphasis is on the continuity. During the run changes of costume or props can be tried out. The music can be left running and the change can be timed exactly to the material. Make sure that all props are used and that any writing is big enough to be seen at the back of the auditorium.

They sing one act and perform dance and drama in the other. The space for this rehearsal should be the largest in the centre and the floor should be marked out to the full dimensions of the stage. If things run to plan there will be time left for notes and polishing. Any notes should be short and to the point. The work should be ready for band call and your actors should be confident and excited about sharing their work.

The Band Call

A band call is an exciting first run-through bringing together most of the elements of the show. By the end of the rehearsal your actors should have a good idea how what they do fits with everyone else.

The floor is marked out in advance to the dimensions that can be expected at the theatre. It will show the positions of the red choir, the blue choir and the band as well as the acting/dancing area downstage. The centre of the stage at the front will be clearly marked. The different numbered backstage areas are also marked.

In the middle of the stage the microphones on stands are set up for the soloists and voices of the characters. At the front there are tables for the sound, director, stage manager, etc. The band call is partly for these people to see how the show fits together. There is sometimes a band with amplification and the musical director. It is usual not to wear costumes but it is useful to use any props.

After a short introduction to the various spaces, everyone in the show goes to their starting positions and the first act is run without a break. It is rare for the rehearsal to stop so if a mistake is made a group is expected to carry on – as they would be expected to do in performance.

During the run it is usual for the teacher who has prepared the drama to join the show director at the front when it is their number. This saves time and enables any notes to be passed on and questions asked.

At the end of the first act the director and the musical director give some brief notes and after a break Act Two is continued. The musicians work a three-hour call and everything has to be fitted into that – notes as well – so there is only one chance to get things right. Rather like the show itself!

The band call reveals how well prepared each centre is. Your centre should be at performance readiness.
If your pre-call rehearsal went to plan your actors should be ready to work with strangers. They will:

- Bring energy and enthusiasm to their work but be still and quiet when they are not the centre of attention.
- Concentrate on what they have to do and watch what others do.
- Hold on to their energy and excitement and put it into the show.
- Work as a team and follow the leaders.
- Follow the backstage instructions at the correct time.
- Be generous to other performers.
- Not worry if mistakes are made.

What you do on band call day

- You are more of an observer than a participant.
- Watch the centre and note problems or changes for later discussion.
- Be available at the front of the performing area during your piece to confer with the director.
- Do not get involved with what happens onstage. It is tempting to jump in and help but it is more important that they take responsibility for what happens as in performance. The more you can let the leaders and the group take on responsibility, the better. Sometimes chaperones and others who are travelling with the centre get tense, overprotective and are sometimes less than generous with other centres. All the adults should share the same attitudes as those you teach your cast.

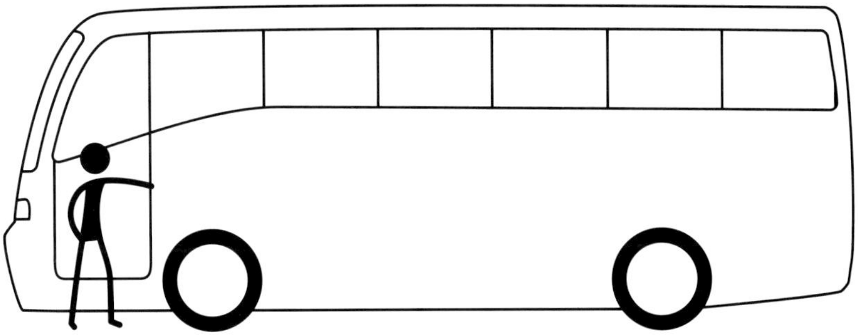

The journey there and back

The action of travelling together helps to bond the pupils and the teachers. They are on a journey together in more ways than one. Encourage the feeling of being a team. A bit of competition is likely but don't let it take over.

After the Band Call

If your show is the next day your notes need to be passed onto the pupils while it is still fresh in their heads. This could be done before getting on the coach. Some coaches have a microphone which they may let you use. By this time the notes should be short. If they are too complicated they are unlikely to be remembered.

TIP
The rule backstage is that if you can see the audience then they can see you.

If your show is a week away you have the opportunity to spend another Saturday giving the notes, reflecting on the band call and making final preparations.

Try to keep a sense of humour and perspective about the work. It is important that the final stages are kept simple. If you approach everything in a positive frame of mind it rubs off onto others. Large-scale productions bring pressure in the final stages but they always have an infectious excitement in performance. Character is revealed in moments of stress and your way of overcoming problems straightforwardly is useful for your actors to see; it's a skill that they can take with them.

Depending on how you work with your group you can continue to make slight changes to the work. This will keep them attentive and creative. They will understand that creating work in the theatre is a controllable form and that it is possible even at this late stage to refine the product.

Band calls and performances are tiring. If your centre has a band call and a show on the same weekend you need to talk about saving energy. Maybe your young people have boundless energy but you need them sharp on performance night.

Show Day

The excitement of the band call was a trial run for the big day. Now comes the time for it to enchant an audience.

Consider your own role on the day, experiencing the event with your company. They will calmer during the day if they feel your reassuring presence. Acknowledge that it is their day. Although your creative work is over, your reaction to what they do is important to them. They would feel terribly let down if you were not interested in seeing the results of your joint work. They need to know that you care about them.

When they arrive at the theatre they may be surprised by the size and scale of the building. The backstage areas and the auditorium are probably different to what they expected. This is the time to rediscover the centre mark on the stage, note the relationship between the stage and the auditorium and discover the route to the dressing room.

Whatever they use as a dressing room it needs to be left as tidy as it was found. Respect for the building and the people who work in it is as important as respecting fellow performers. Costumes, food and drink are stowed and the company assembles for a talk by the theatre manager. Theatres can be dangerous places so the health and safety procedure is necessary, as is discovering the routes of exit from the theatre in the unlikely event of an emergency. During this day it is safer for your cast to move around together and take toilet or water breaks under the direction of staff.

The director of the show uses this time to point out the different areas of the stage and to invite groups up to rehearse some elements of the show. This is when your cast begin to own the stage; not to be overawed by the building, and sense that they can send their performance to the back row.

Large numbers of young people gathered together in such a situation are very bubbly. This is good; you want your cast to feel the excitement of the day. What you don't want is for them to waste their energy on unnecessary activity. Encourage them to drink water. The lights are hot and dehydration could be a problem. There is a lot to deal with. They may be anxious about their performance, perhaps nervous of the size of the building and the restlessness around them. They need focus and reassurance from the professionals. It also helps if they know how the day is going to work. What they may not realise is that many other professionals are working on the production. There is a stage manager who will call the show, staff who are assisting changeover of props and costume at the side of the stage, the theatre's full-time professional crew, the lighting designer and operator, the sound company, follow spot operators and the musicians. All these people need to be coordinated to work smoothly together.

After a break for lunch it is time for the final rehearsal. This is the first time that the lighting and sound operators have seen the show and they have to be ready to serve the show. As with the band call the cast focus on their onstage and offstage jobs. They have to cope with space, the curtain, the differing lighting levels and the routes backstage.

After the final rehearsal there is time for the director and the musical director to give their notes. These are usually short but sometimes the whole cast may need to rehearse a moment that involves them all.

The cast are also rehearsed in taking applause. Each centre takes its bow. You can tell a lot about a group by watching how they bow. There should be a measured walk down where everyone moves as one, a leader in the middle who checks that everyone is in place before taking a bow with which everyone synchronises. A smile is important. It is interesting to see the actor rather than the character at this moment – to see their delight, their uninhibited pleasure at the applause. This is a moment to savour for a performer because it is the culmination of the work, and why would you rush that?

There has to be time to eat and drink and get into costumes – hopefully a time as well to rest. You may want to give some final notes of your own. This has been a year-long journey, a gathering together of so many different skills. To have stayed on that journey and to feel ready to perform is exhilarating. There ought to be a sense of completion and fulfilment. Enjoy this moment with them and let those thoughts remain unsaid until the following week.

TIP

If someone is very nervous show them how to breathe in to counts of 9 and out to 11.

Adrenalin plays a part at this time as they near the performance. Nervousness is a natural response. It is a good thing as it means that you care about what you do. Most performers experience nerves. The solution is to use them to focus a sharper intensity into the performance. If someone is really affected by their nervousness – and children can be susceptible to the group feeling going on around them – then show them how to take a deep breath and control themselves by breathing out slowly.

By the 15-minute call they are ready to take up their positions for beginners. Are they ready for performance – are they vocally and physically prepared and focused for what follows? Perhaps you have a simple game to help them focus on the work ahead. You could ask them to think privately of someone to whom they will dedicate their performance.

And the show begins. They cope with whatever happens because they have to. Your organisation has prepared them to take things in their stride and work for each other. You have given them real life skills in a place that requires discipline, teamwork and the amazing thrill of achieving what they set out to do.

After the performance praise them for their work – if possible individually. Your response and the response of their parents will be important to them. They will want to know what you thought of them and to know that they succeeded. Your genuine pleasure at what they did is something special you can give them – the gift of validation.

After the Show

The following week you can look back and share time talking about the experience and what other people thought about it. What was the feedback, the reactions of family and friends? What did they, the cast, think about how well they did? What about the whole term of preparation. Was that enjoyable? Was the journey worth it? What did they learn?

Remind them of the layers of preparation they made.

- Understanding the plot.
- Building a character.
- Making the story work in the space.
- Fitting the story to the music.
- Working on the details to each section.
- Bringing it to life through movement.
- Looking at entrances and exits.
- Making the conflict powerful.
- Finding the big moment.
- Working on attitude.
- Dealing with the audience.

It is important to draw a line under the event but before moving on reflect on what the process was about. Sometimes it is good to take things more slowly and think them over before they are gone. Good theatre leaves an impression, a memory, perhaps a changed understanding, and it takes time to appreciate this.

Maybe the experience was not a positive one for everybody. Stress the positive aspect of what has been learnt. It is easy to find fault with things and this is a place to hear any complaints, but keep a sense of balance and remind them of the new skills they have discovered. You hope that they will want to go on a new journey with you, find new skills and work on fresh stories and characters.

And then it is time to move on. Return to process work and see it as a continuum. The process skills they learnt at the beginning of the year were ways of raising the individual skill of each pupil. The production skills that come later are connected; the self and the group, the individual skill and the story that the group works on. Each informs each other.

The work is never completed because there is always something new to learn about the theatre, about life and the world and about your character and who you are.

Summary for February to July work

Exploring the story and the characters.

Casting the play and ensuring that everyone has something meaningful to do.

Putting the action on the stage and encouraging creative input from the actors.

Exploring the work in space and time, sound and movement, conflict, the big moment, attitude and the audience.

Preparing for and participating in the Band Call.

Performing to the audience.

Getting feedback on the production and moving the work on to a new area of process work.

Appendix A

GOOD WORK IN PERFORMANCE

There are high standards to be met week to week and in performance.

The work is accomplished, the characters and stories believable, the ideas interesting and varied and there is attention to detail. We care about what happens to the characters and it seems natural and truthful. It is creative and balanced between moments of humour and seriousness.

The performers gleam; as a team they possess confidence, passion, flexibility and discipline. They enjoy participating and we can see this in the way they work. They are well motivated and hungry to learn.

Offstage they focused. They are generous and work as a team. They are well organised and understand theatre discipline.

The use of space is always interesting with attention paid to alignment, height, depth, width and sightlines.

Soloists and leaders are well chosen and prepared for their tasks.

They take real pleasure in their work and in our reaction to it. They are committed, enthusiastic and energetic and prepare properly at home.

The performance is continuous and professional. There are no wasted moments or performers superfluous to the action.

It is clear that the audience has been thought about as part of the preparation.

Technical matters have been considered and there is effective use of costumes, properties, lighting, sound and stage design.

Ideas from the pupils are in the work – they own the material and the space.

There is variety of mood and atmosphere and strong emotions. Conflict plays an important part in the story.

The performance seems to pass by quickly and sometimes we and they are under its spell and can lose ourselves in the work.

Most pupils appreciate differences between styles and genres and use them in the work.

Watching the performance charms our emotions. We learn something new. The experience enhances our life. We shall remember it for a long time. Sometimes it is genuinely inspiring.

Centre Directors, teachers and chaperones are supportive of others and exemplify the above qualities themselves. They are open minded and improve their work from year to year.

APPENDIX B
List of Opposites

ACTIONS

accept	refuse
admit	deny
attack	defend
blame	praise
bless	curse
borrow	lend
build	destroy
come	go
demand	supply
find	lose
gather	distribute
grant	refuse
help	hinder
hunger	thirst
inhale	exhale
question	answer
scatter	collect
sow	reap
take	give

SPACE

advance	retreat
approach	depart
ascend	descend
backward	forward
begin	end
below	above
broad	narrow
clockwise	anti-clockwise
close	distant
conceal	reveal
enter	exit
expand	contract
first	last
fuse	separate
hasten	dawdle
horizontal	vertical
increase	decrease
internal	external
left	right
lengthen	shorten
less	more
low	high
maximum	minimum
odd	even
restrict	free
slow	fast
stand	lie

PHYSICAL ATTRIBUTES

abundant	scarce
ancient	modern
artificial	natural
beautiful	ugly
best	worst
big	small
bitter	sweet
blunt	sharp
bright	dull
clear	vague
cold	hot
common	rare
curved	straight
dark	light
deep	shallow
dry	wet
dusk	dawn
empty	full
fat	thin
fresh	stale
full	empty
land	sea
light	dark
minority	majority
often	seldom
permanent	temporary
plentiful	scarce
rigid	pliable
rough	smooth
singular	plural
solid	liquid
transparent	opaque

HUMAN QUALITIES

absence	presence
alive	dead
asleep	awake
bad	good
bold	timid
calm	troubled
captive	free
cautious	impulsive
clever	stupid
courteous	rude
cruel	kind
cunning	simple
dainty	clumsy
defeat	victory
despair	hope
disease	health
dismal	cheerful
early	late
easy	difficult
economise	waste
fail	succeed
forget	remember
frank	secretive
friend	enemy
generous	mean
guilty	innocent
happy	sad
hero	coward
humble	proud
intentional	accidental
lazy	energetic
love	hate
loyal	untrustworthy
master	servant
optimist	pessimist
peace	war
poverty	wealth
private	public
rich	poor
right	wrong

serious	trivial
simple	complicated
sober	drunk
speak	listen
strong	weak
truth	lie
virtue	vice
wise	foolish

APPENDIX C

Theatrical Styles and Conventions

There are a variety of theatrical styles used in theatre and drama. These include:

Comedy
Comedy of manners
Comedy of situation
Farce
Romantic comedy
Satiric and ironic comedy
Stand-up and observational comedy
Drama
Epic theatre
Fantasy/Grotesque
Melodrama
Morality play
Musical theatre
Parody
Pantomime
Physical theatre
Political theatre
Popular theatre
Tragedy
Tragicomedy

Absurdist – Life makes no sense. Chaos rules when we try to make sense.

Expressionistic – Truth is distorted unrealistically to reveal something deeper and more meaningful.

Commedia dell'arte – Masked stock characters interpret life through improvisation of plot and incorporation of planned routines.

Melodrama – Good triumphs over evil with an unlikely plot, stock characters and over-sentimentalised stock characters.

Naturalism – A highly detailed and truthful depiction of life.

Postmodernism – A jumble of thoughts and feelings juxtaposing a wide range of theatre, art and film forms.

Puppetry – Objects become people.

APPENDIX D
Music for Mood or Atmosphere

Happy
Girls and Boys in Love
- The Rumblestrips
Do Your Thing - Basement Jacks
You Made me so Very Happy
- Blood Sweat and Tears

Cheerful
Mr Blue Sky - ELO
Waterloo Sunset - The Kinks
Happy Together - The Turtles

Hope/Optimism
If I Can Dream - Elvis Presley
One Day I'll Fly Away - Craig Armstrong
Don't Stop Me Now - Queen

Peaceful
What a Wonderful World - Louis Armstrong
Adiemus - Karl Jenkins
Here Comes the Sun - The Beatles

Romantic
I Will - Paul McCartney
Have I Told You Lately? - Van Morrison
Cornerstone - Artic Monkeys

Longing
The Look of Love - Diana Krall
Romeo and Juliet - Prokoviev
The Man I Love - Billie Holiday

Regret
You've lost that Lovin' Feeling
- The Righteous Brothers
If I Could Turn Back Time - Cher
I'm Still Breathing - Katy Perry

Unrequited Love
You're Beautiful - James Blunt
Teenage Dirtbag - Wheatus
Shiver - Coldplay

Stand aside
New York New York - Frank Sinatra
Don't Rain on My Parade - Barbra Streisand

Lust
Sexual Healing - Marvin Gaye
I'm so Excited - The Pointer Sisters
Light My Fire - Jose Feliciano

Patriotic
Nimrod - Elgar
Jupiter - Holst
Zadok the Priest - Handel

Noble
Crown Imperial - Walton
Pomp and Circumstance - Elgar
I Was Glad - Parry

Heroic
The Untouchables - Ennio Morricone
Gladiator - Hans Zimmer
Anthem Part 2 - The Truman Show

Angst
My Generation - The Who
I Predict a Riot - Kaiser Chiefs
School's Out - Alice Cooper

Sad
Adagio for Strings - Barber
Everybody Hurts - REM
Vocalise - Rachmaninov

Haunting
Mad World - Tears for Fears
Hurt - Johnny Cash
Breathe Me - Sia

Loss
The Living Years - Mike and the Mechanics
I Still Believe - Miss Saigon
Schindler's List theme - John Williams

Despair
Adagio Symphony No 5 - Mahler
The Winter's End - Liam O'Flynn
Symphony No 5 - Tchaikovsky

Contemplative
Everyone's Gotta Learn Sometime - Beck
Kyrie Eleison - Stellamara
What's Going on? - Marvin Gaye

Ethereal
In Paradisum - Durufle
Some Where over the Rainbow - Eva Cassidy
The Lark Ascending - Vaughan Williams

Getting Older
Old Friends - Simon and Garfunkel
Brickbat - Billy Bragg
Veronica - Elvis Costello

Scary
Lux Aeterna - Clint Mansell
Every Breath You Take - The Police
4th Symphony - Shostakovich

Declaring
Piano Concerto No 2 - Rachmaninov
Try a Little Tenderness - Otis Redding
Ain't No Mountain High Enough - The Supremes and the Four Tops

Looking back
Fireflies - Owl City
I Will Always Love You - Whitney Houston
It Was a Very Good Year - Frank Sinatra

Reconciliation
Blowing in the Wind - Bob Dylan
A Song For You - Donny Hathaway
Children will Listen - Stephen Sondheim

Foreboding
The Half Killed - Dario Marianelli
Disarm - Smashing Pumpkins
Misery - Maroon 5

Stand Up
I Will Survive - Gloria Gaynor
I'm Still Standing - Elton John
I Still Believe - Miss Saigon

Childhood
Le Redecouverte - Yann Tierson
Unwritten - Natasha Bedingfield
April Come She Will - Paul Simon

There is a wide range of books on drama, theatre and young people. The most influential upon this book have been...

Impro: Improvisation and the Theatre by Keith Johnstone
Impro for Storytellers: Theatresports and the Art of Making Things Happen by Keith Johnstone
Laban for Actors and Dancers: Putting Laban's Movement Theory into Practice – A Step-by-step Guide by Jean Newlove
Laban for All by Jean Newlove and John Dalby
Building A Character by Constantin Stanislavski

Acknowledgements

Many people have contributed to the creation of this book, not least the many pupils and teachers that it has been my pleasure to work with over the years. An early influence was a lecturer when I was training to be a teacher, Brian Watkins, who first invited me to think outside the box. He proposed, radically for those times, that the school play should be performed with the audience on the stage and the performers on the floor. Donald Walker who, as director of the now defunct Curtain Theatre, created a unique space that existed solely to teach how theatre works. It is sadly missed by those who knew it. I learnt a lot from his gentle diplomacy and can-do experience. I owe an enormous debt to the Russian professor, theatre director, teacher and film maker, Mikhail Mokeyev, with whom I had the privilege of working on several occasions. He taught me what it truly means to be *in the moment* in performance and generously shared many of his working methods. He explained to me that the Stanislavski system was explained to him by his professor in the time that it took one metro train to leave the station and the next to arrive. I cannot fail to be impressed by a man who begins each day by pouring cold water over himself.

Over 20 years I have been a sporadic pupil of Jean Newlove who worked with Rudolph Laban in the 40s and then with Joan Littlewood. Her devotion to the true use of Laban's theories is inspiring to a director.

I am also grateful to Sue Colgrave who has worked with me on many large-scale productions and who read and commented on the first draft of this book.

Finally, my love of ensemble was developed by the National Youth Theatre, a wonderful organisation that has had a huge impact on the lives of many people who work in the performing arts industry, and many others who don't.